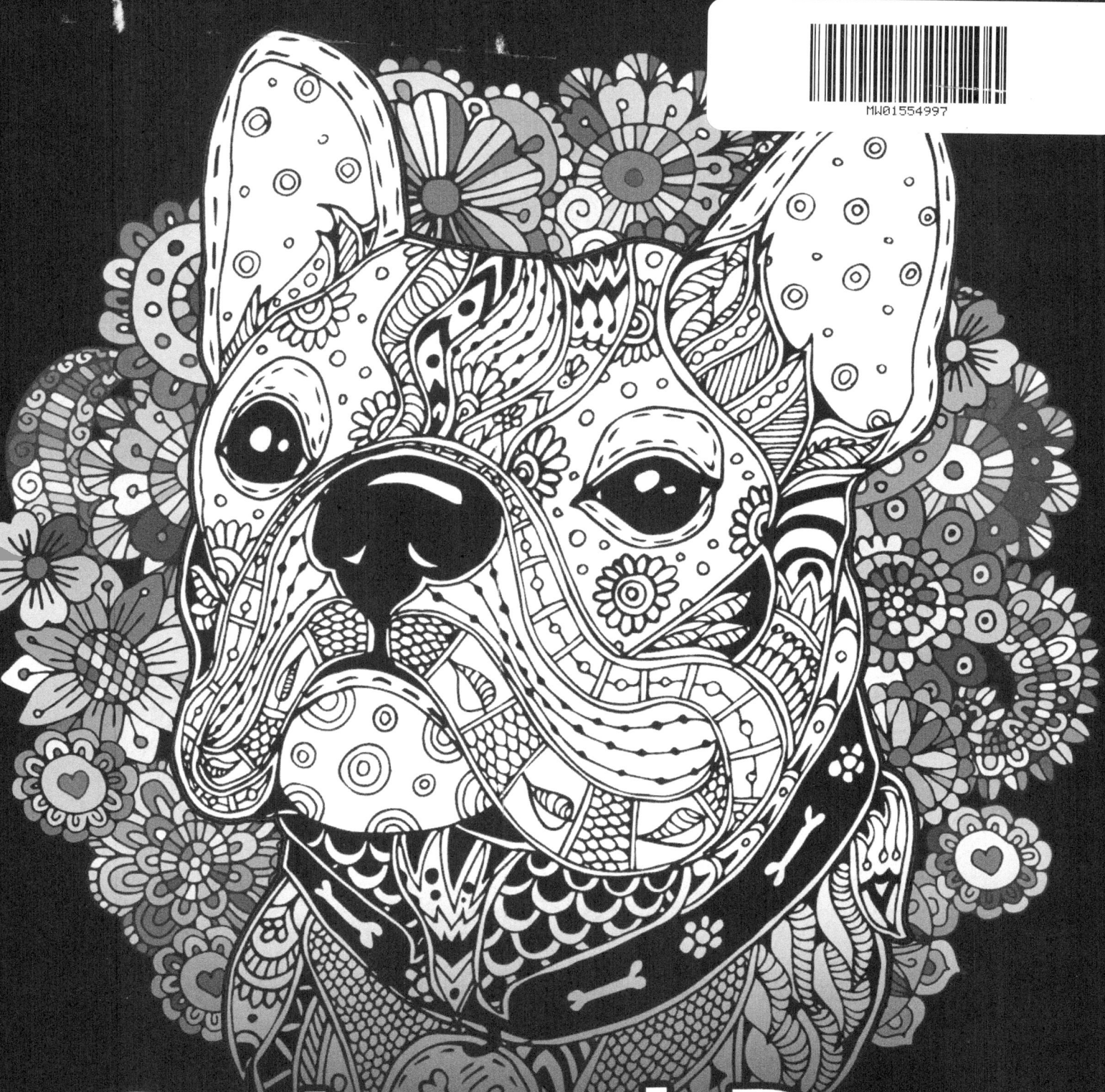

Cat and Dog
COLORING BOOK

Designs for relaxation and mindfuness

Copyright: Published in the United States

Published 2017

All rights reserved.

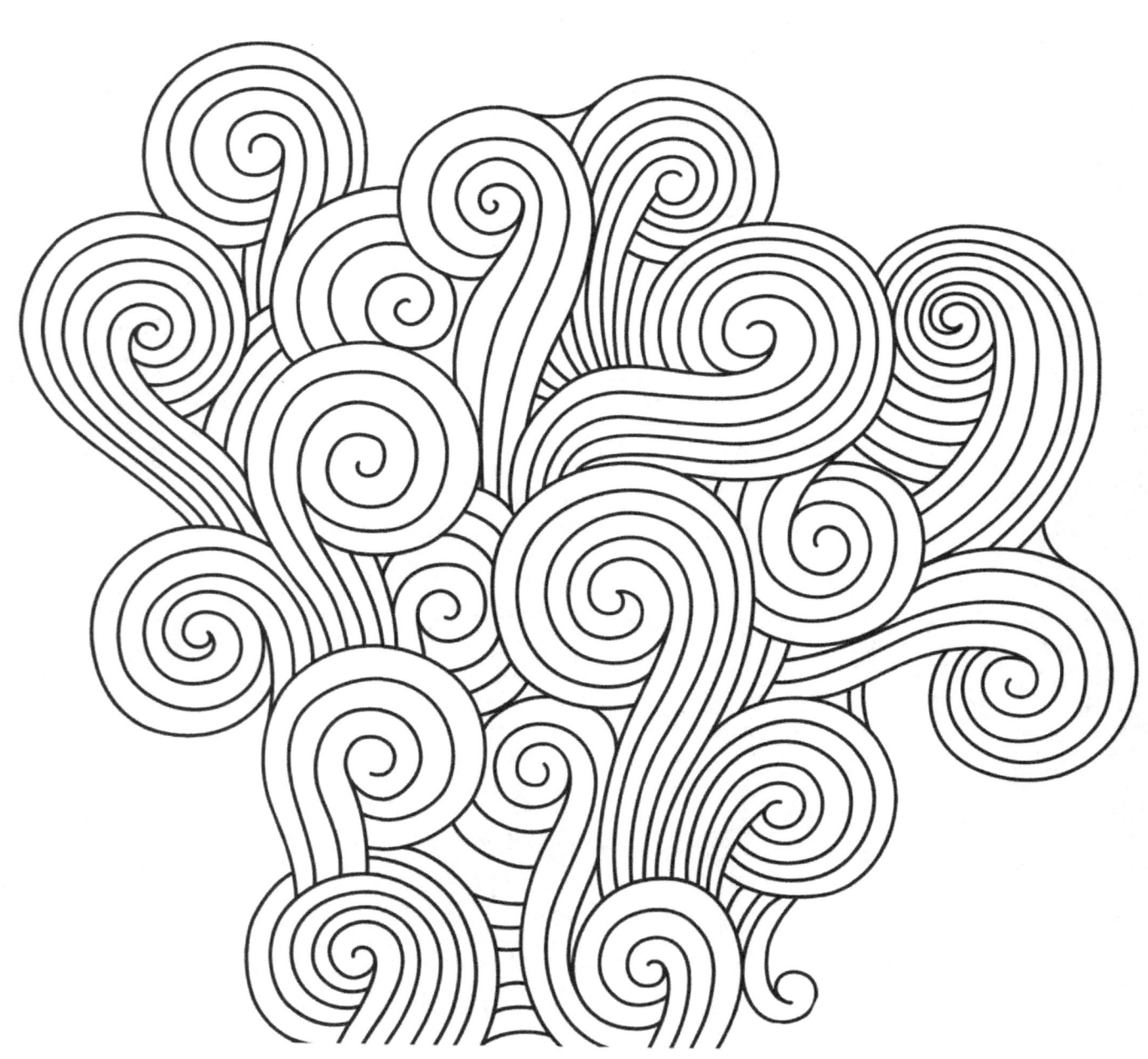

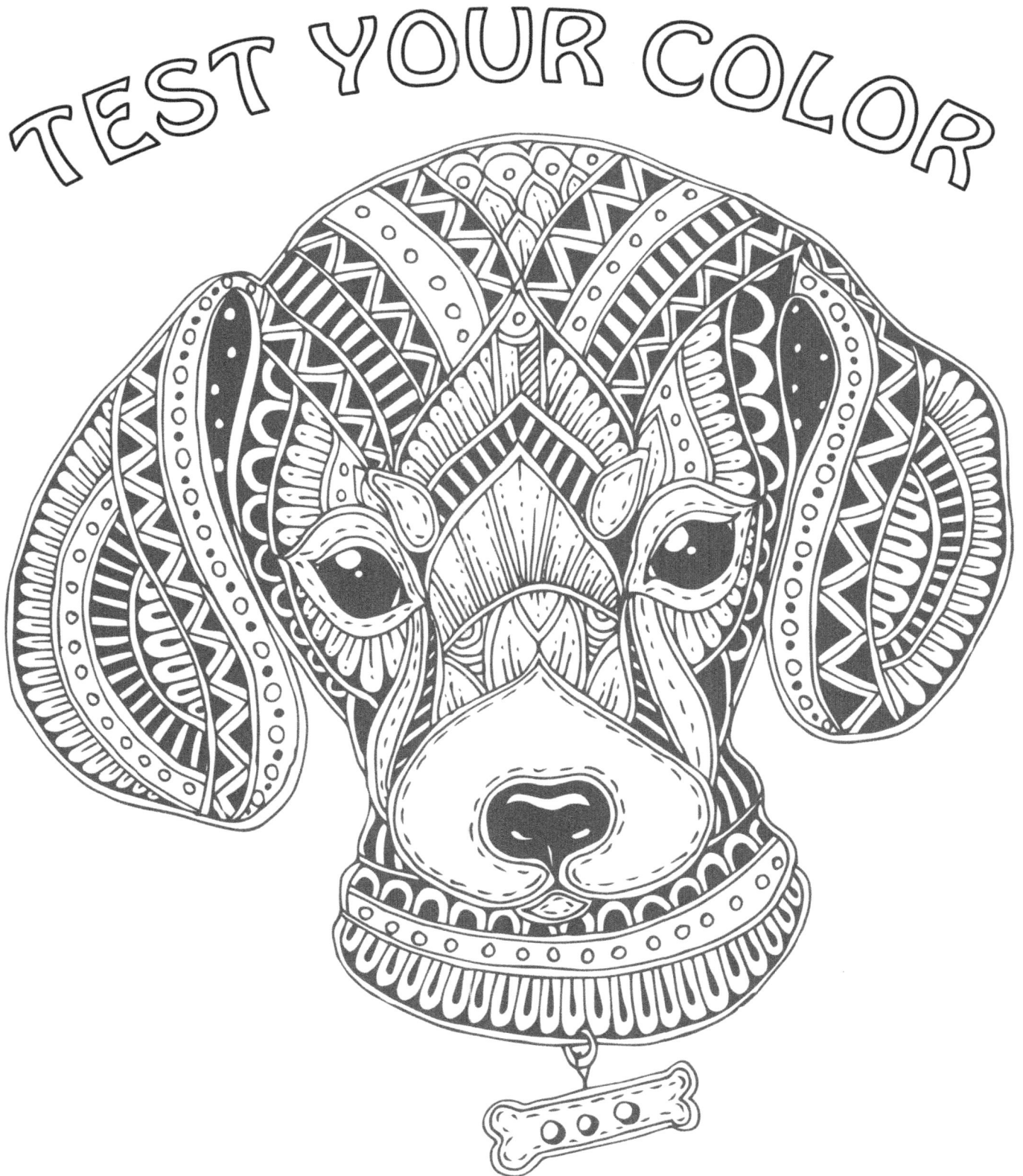

1.

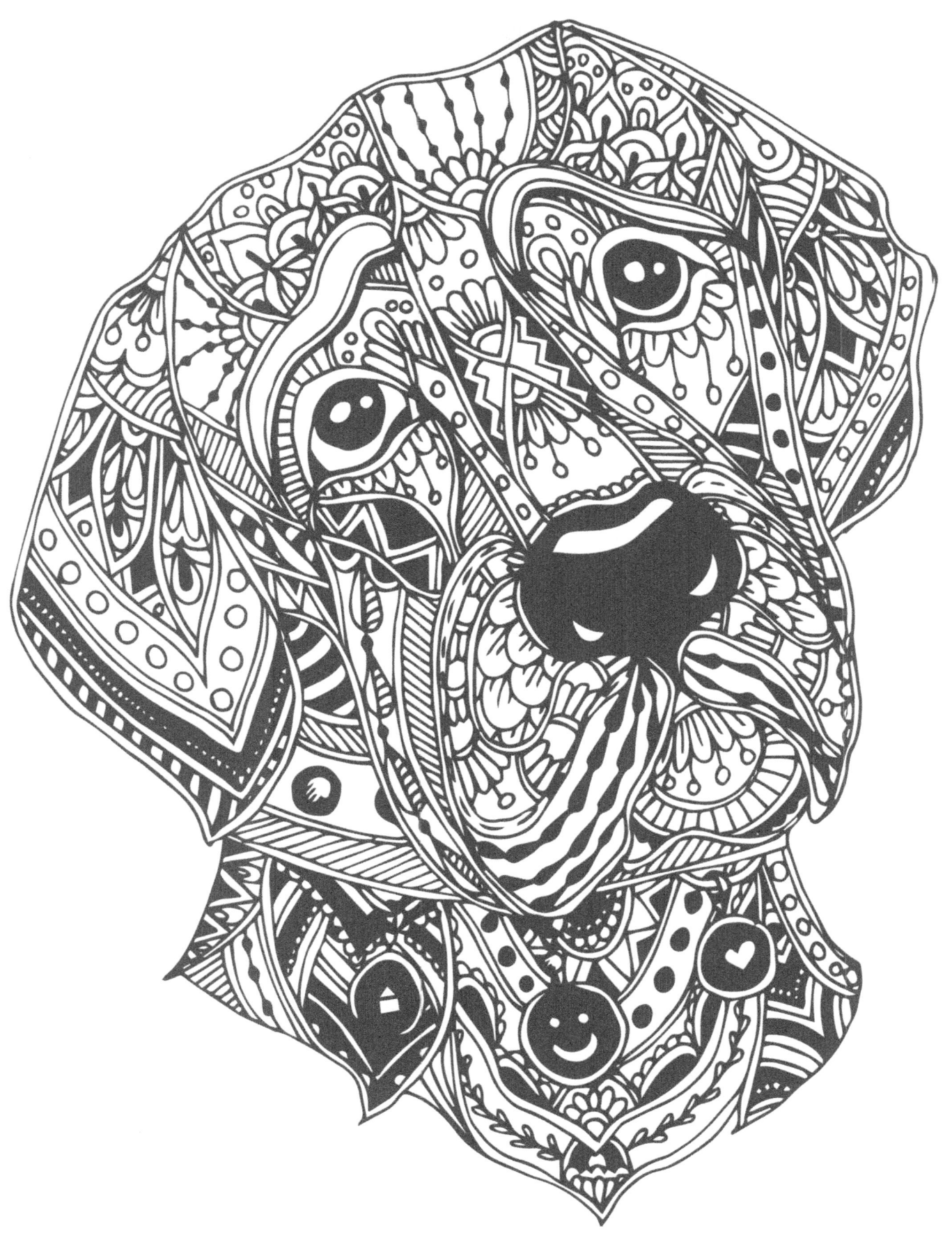

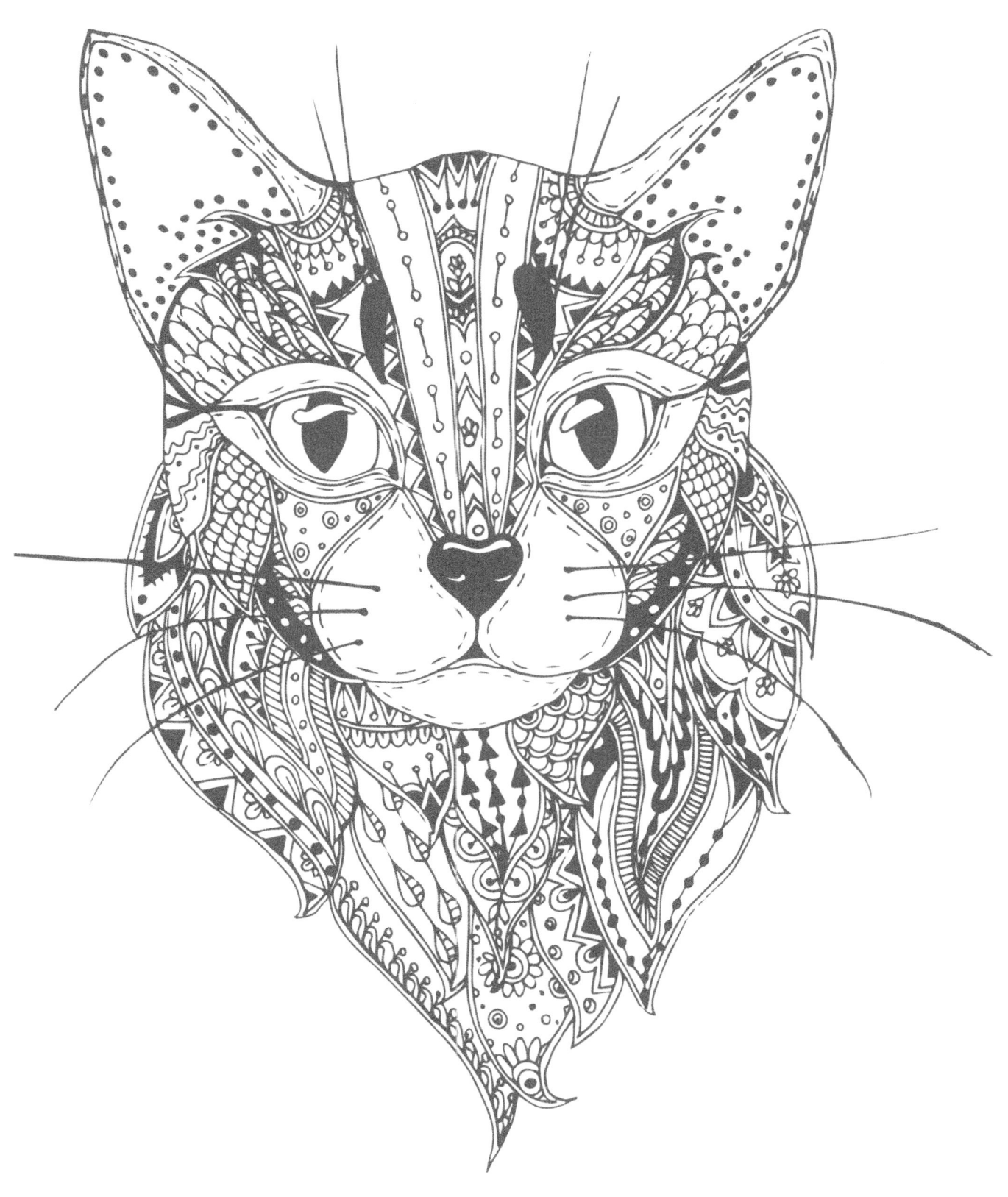

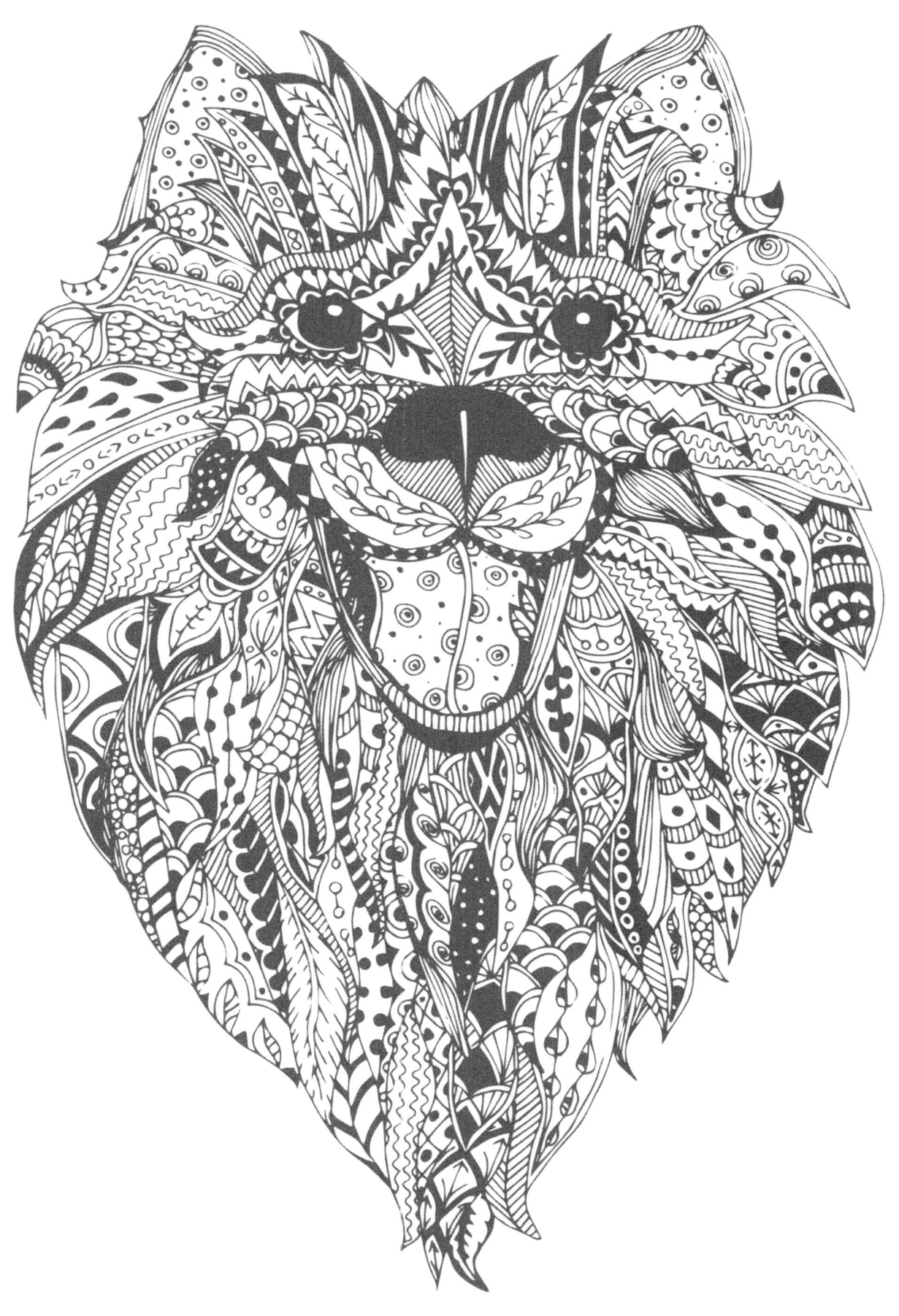

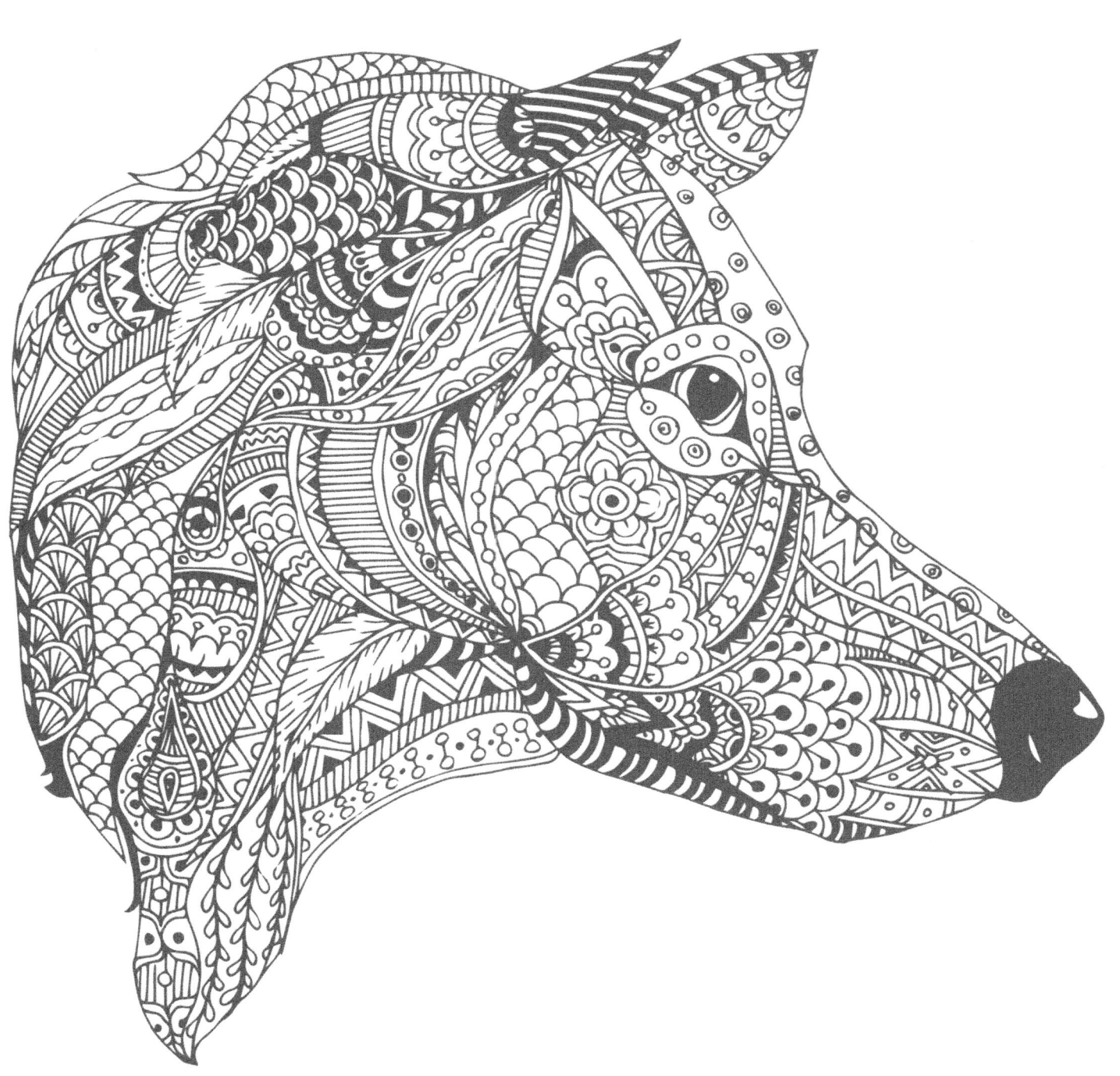

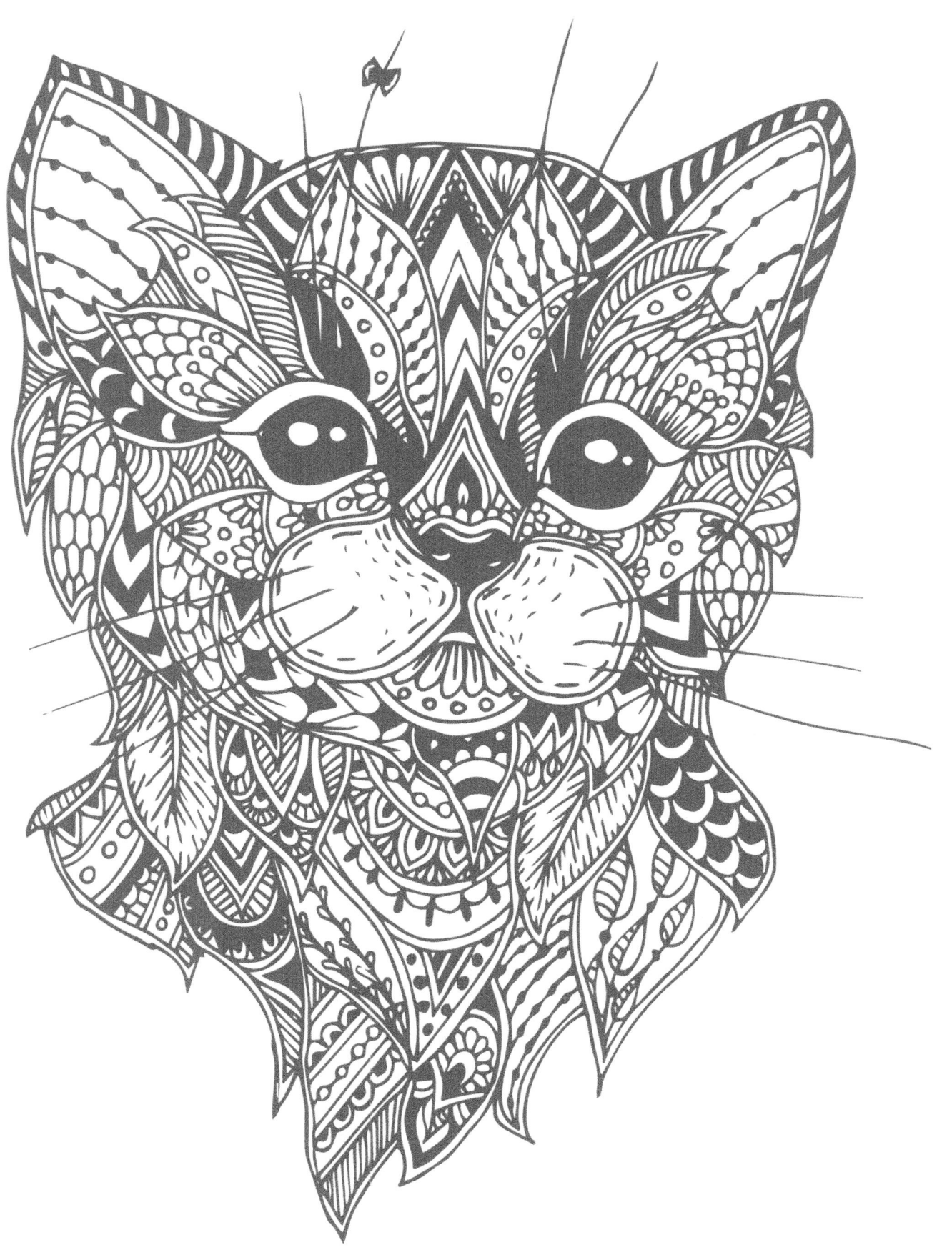

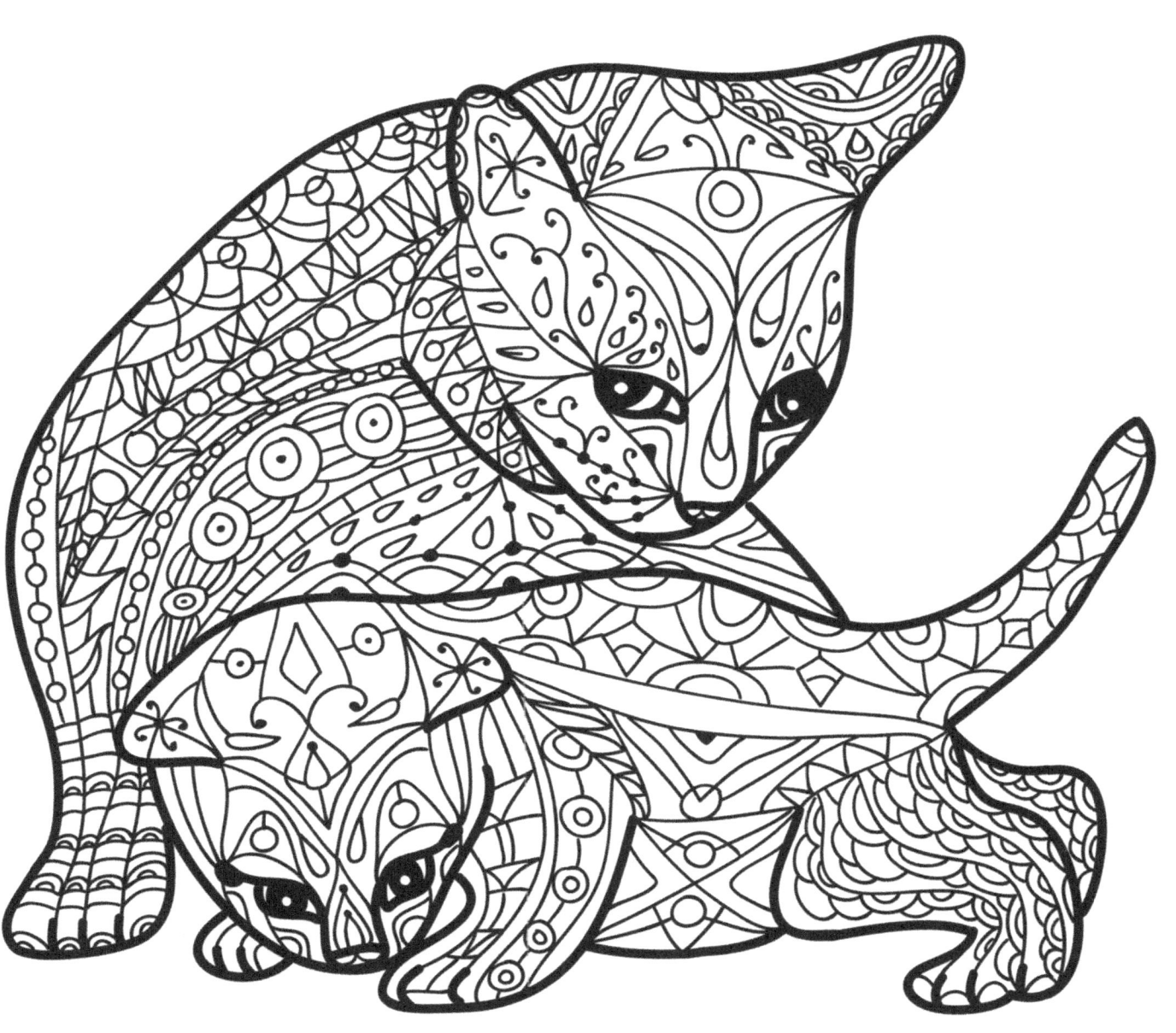

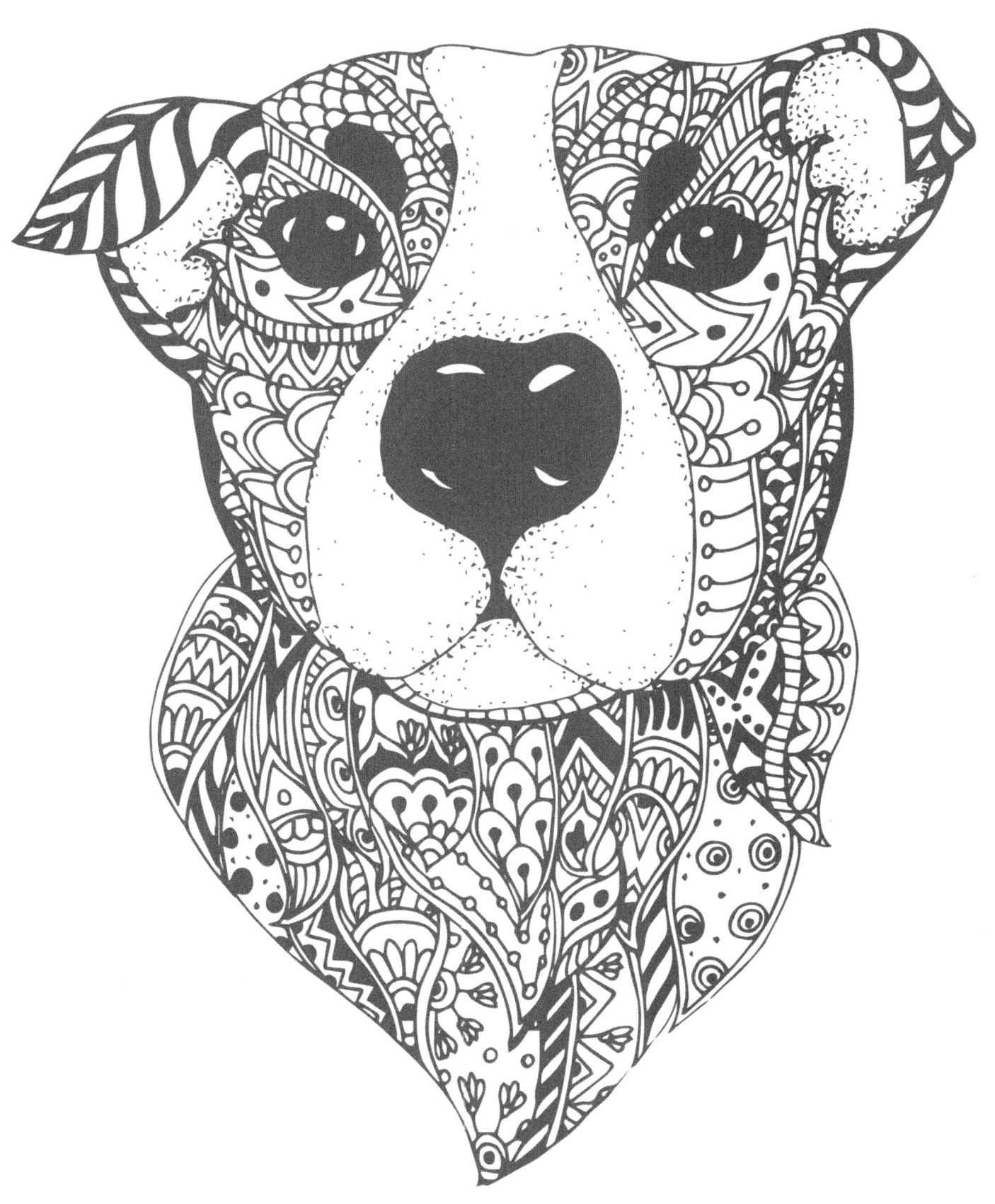

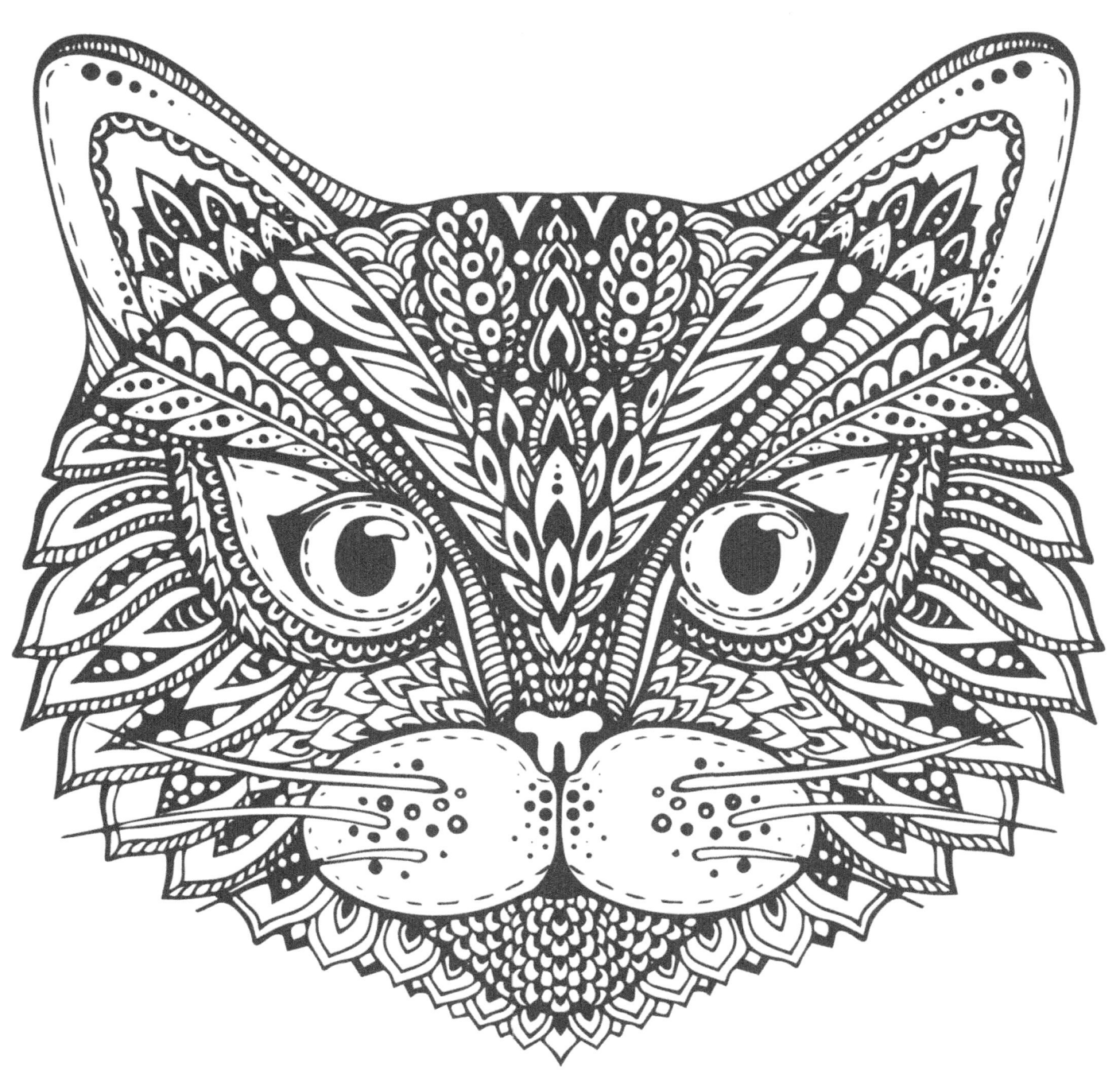

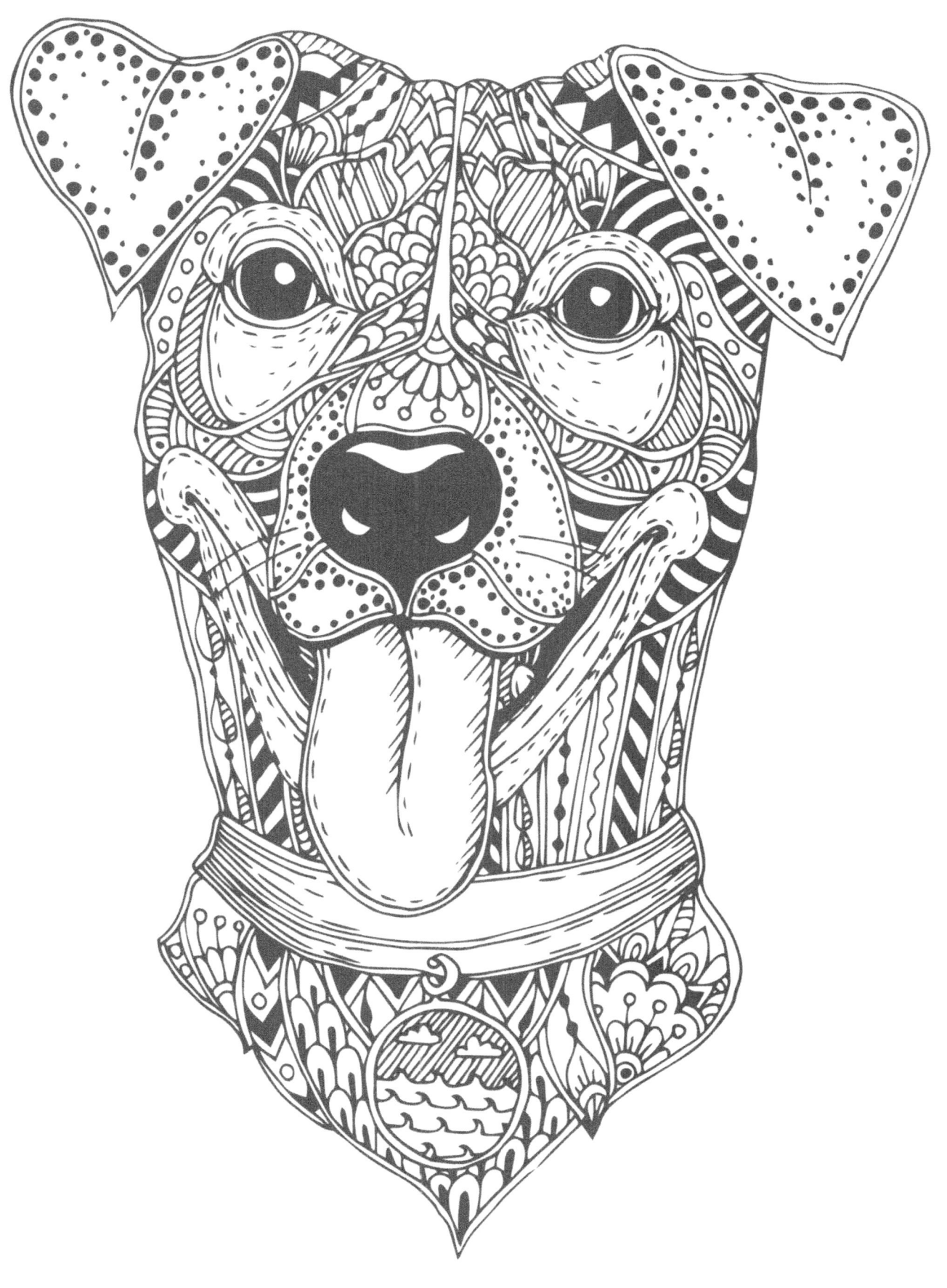

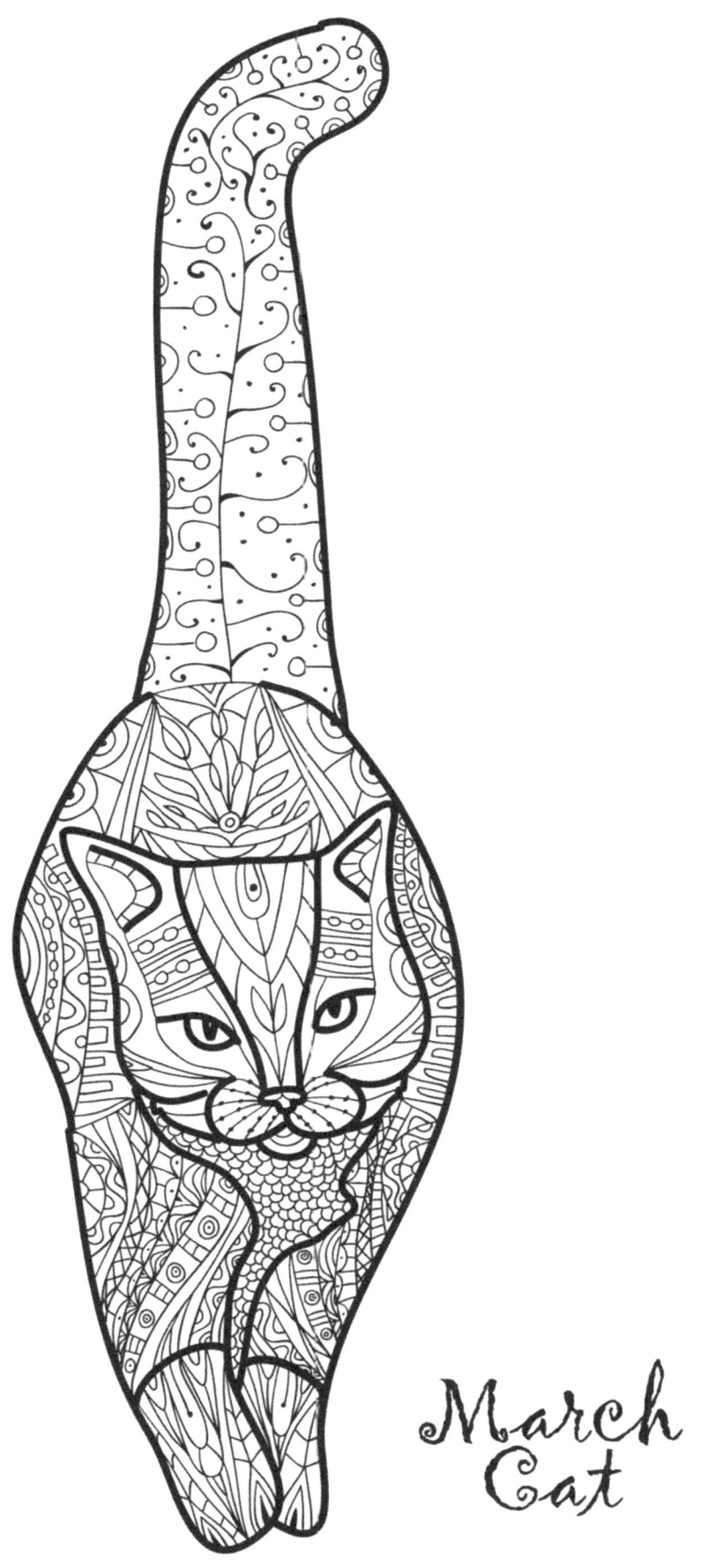

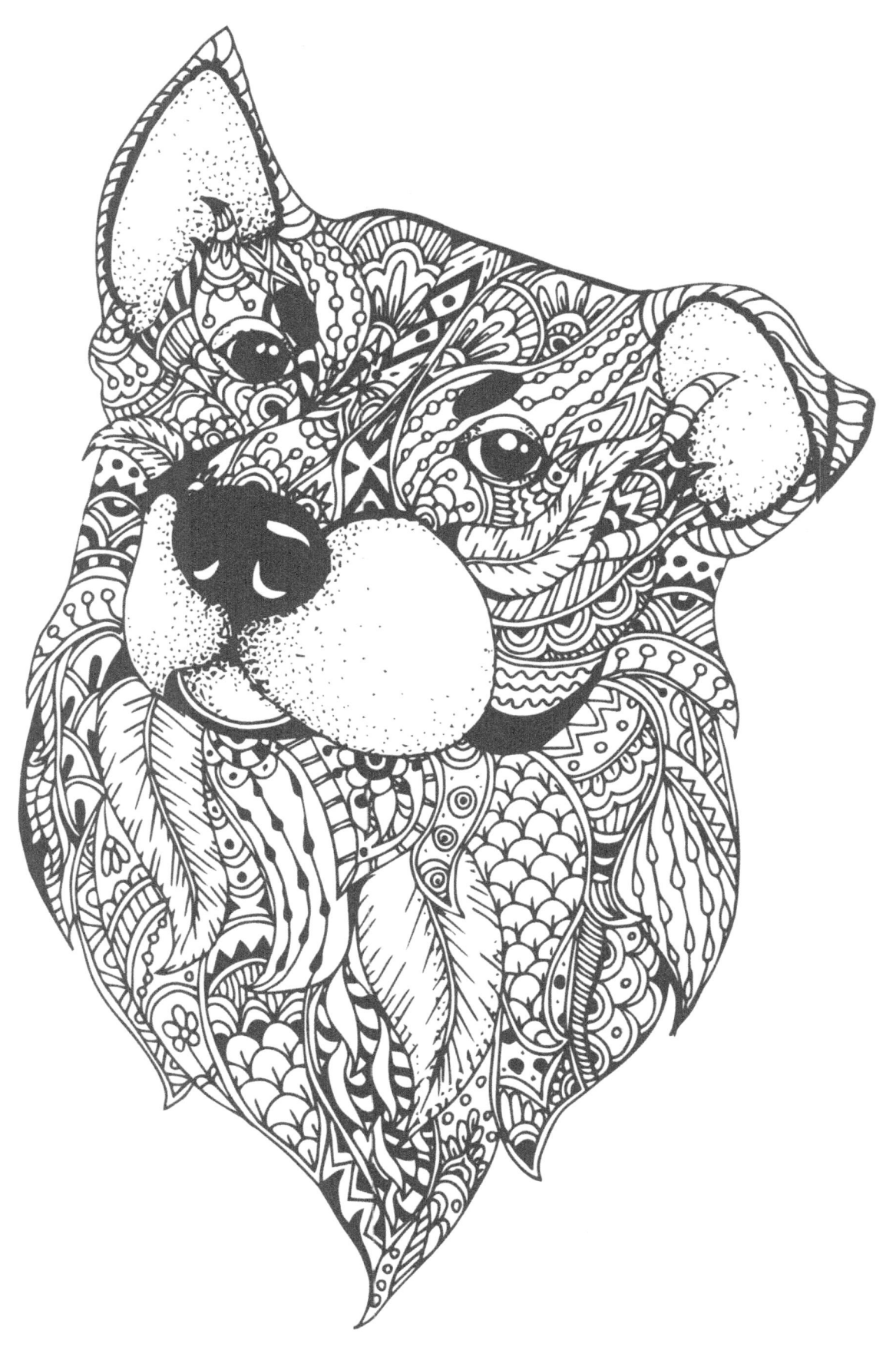

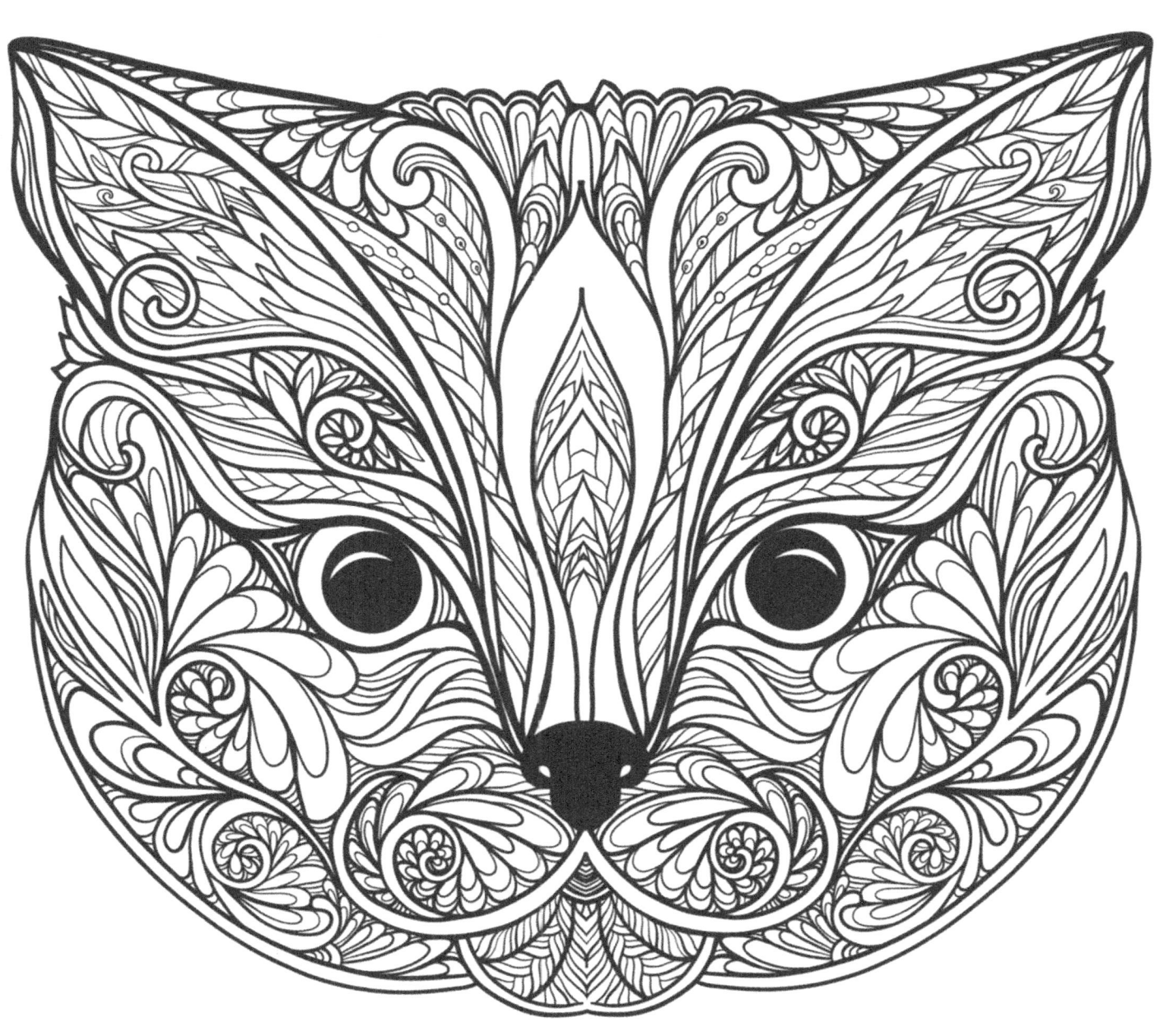

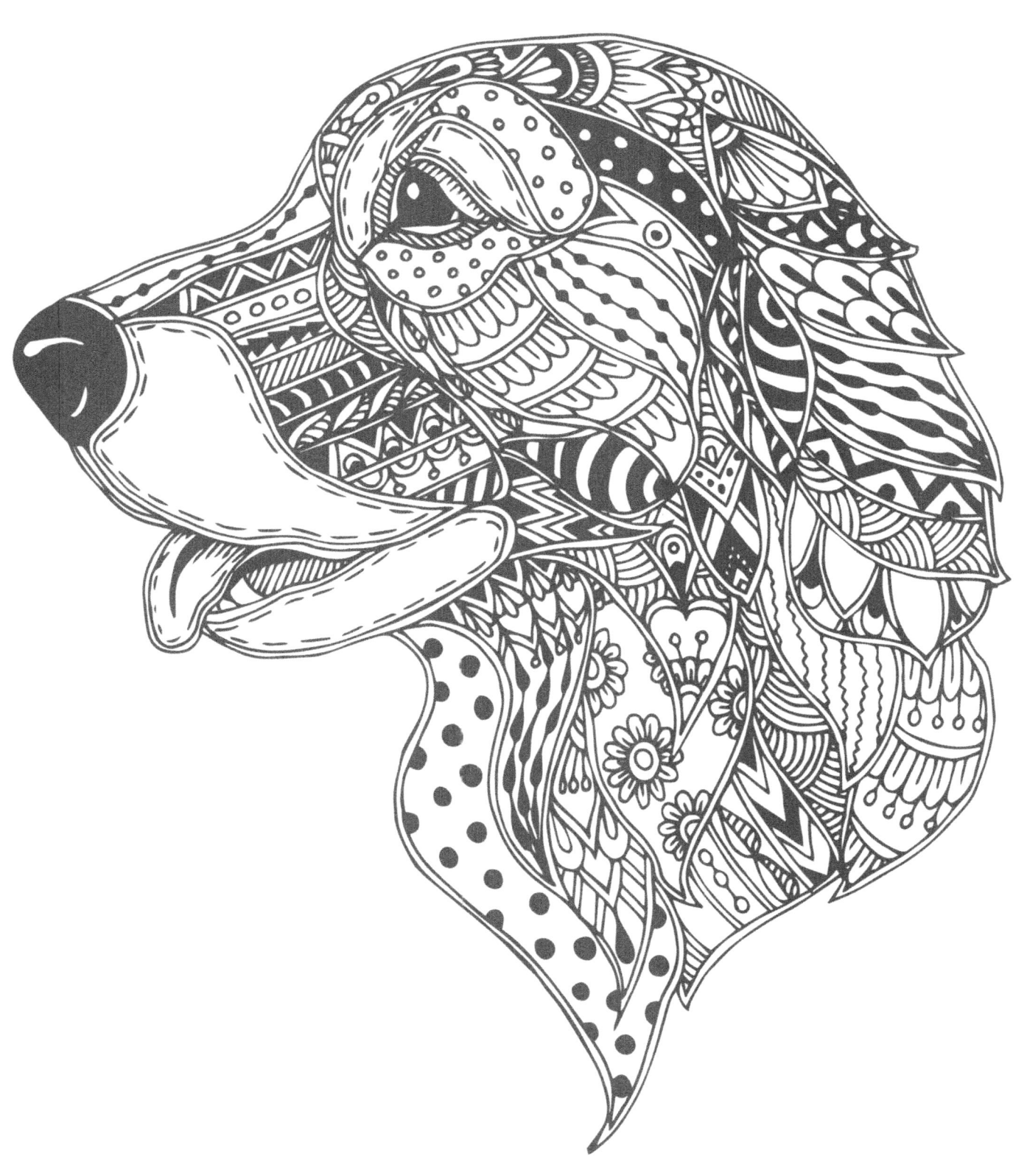

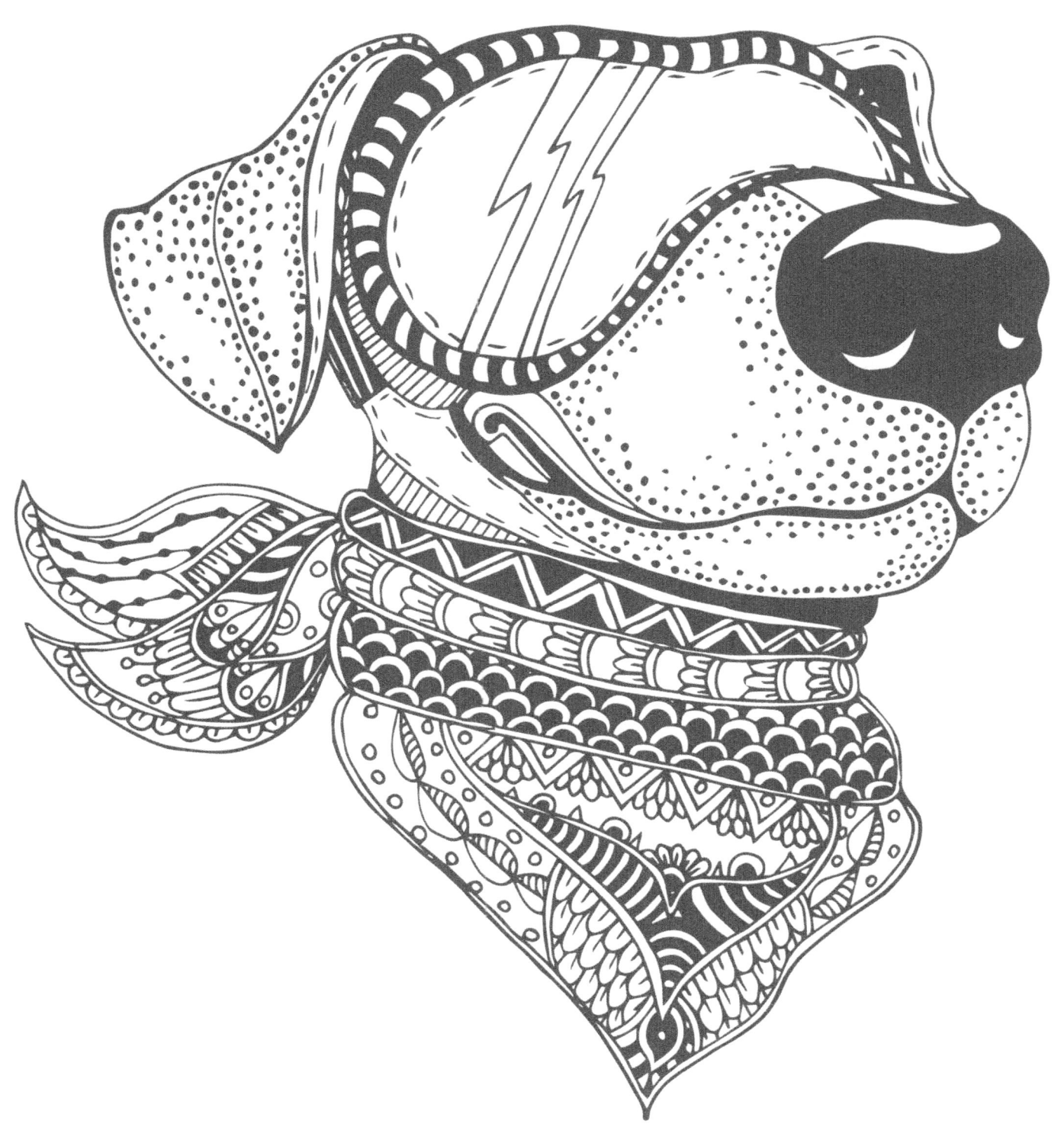

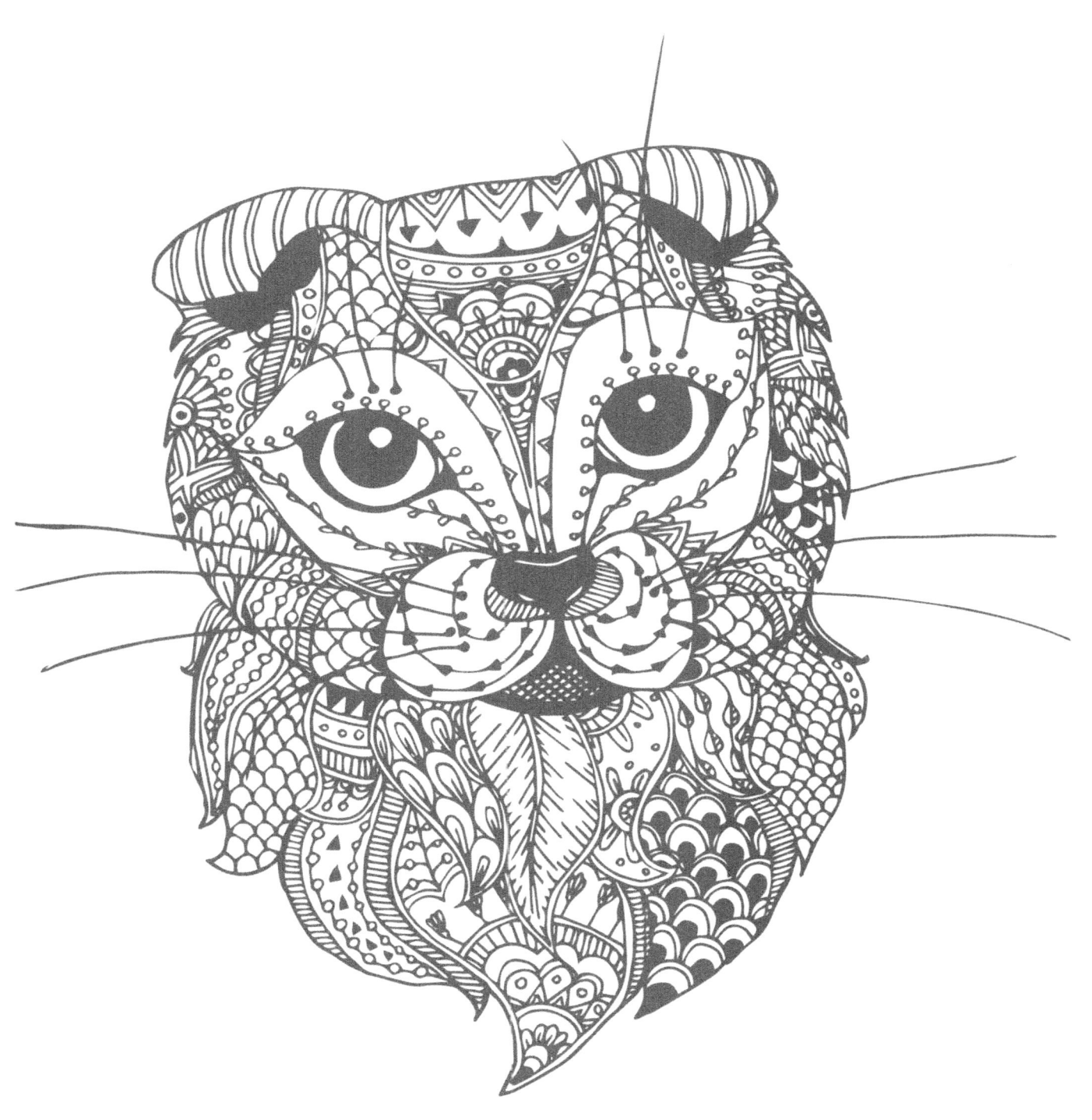

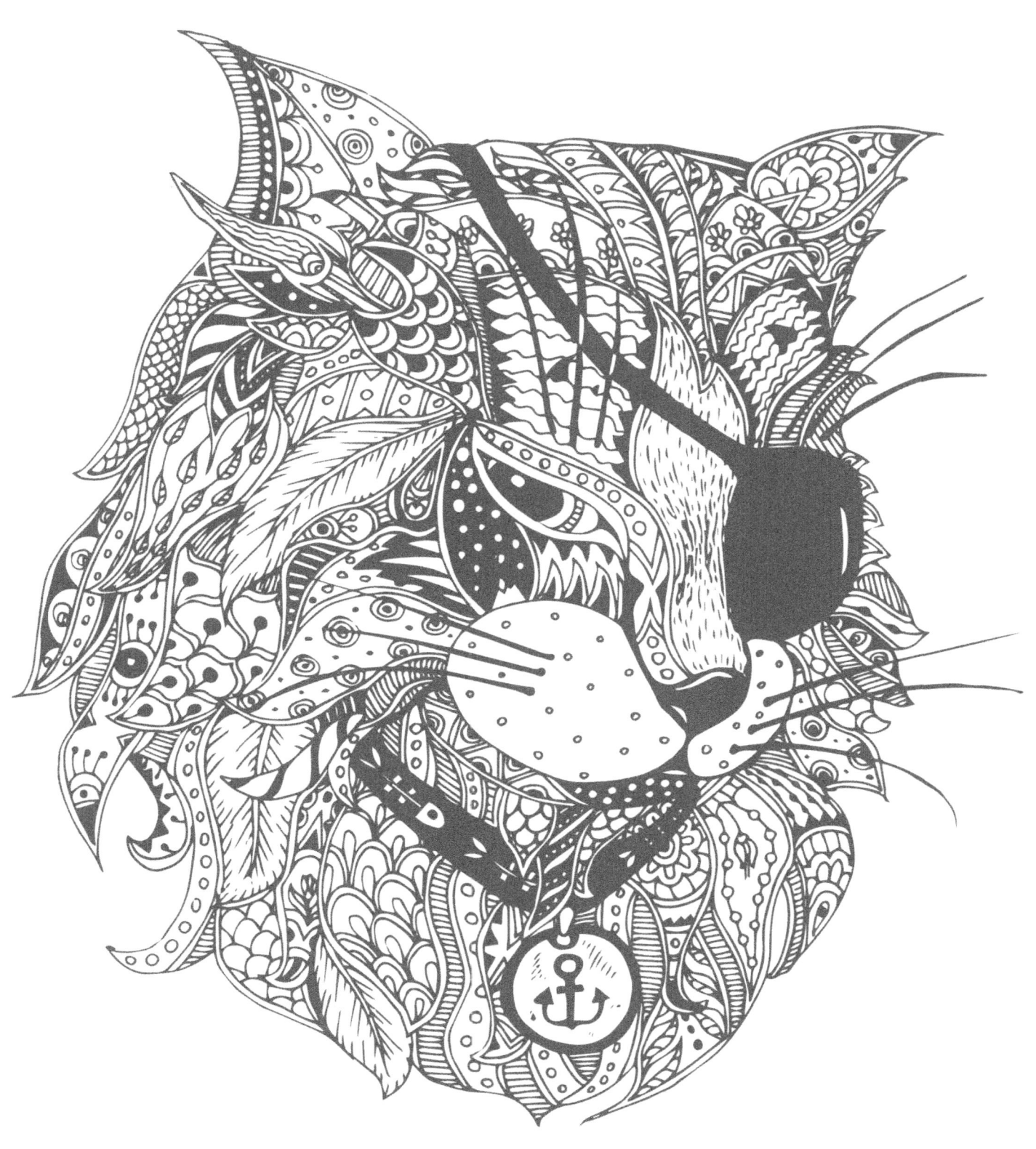

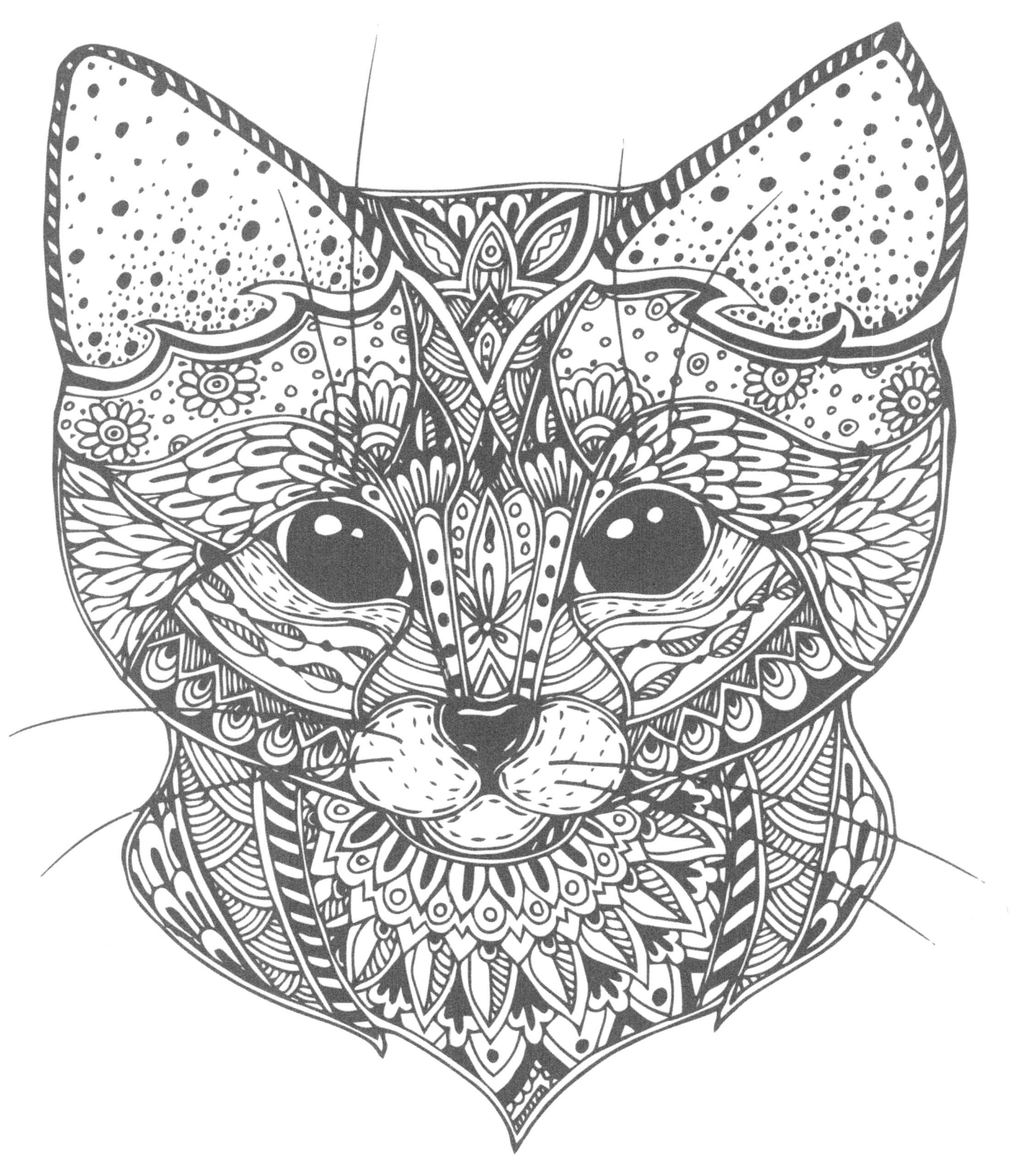

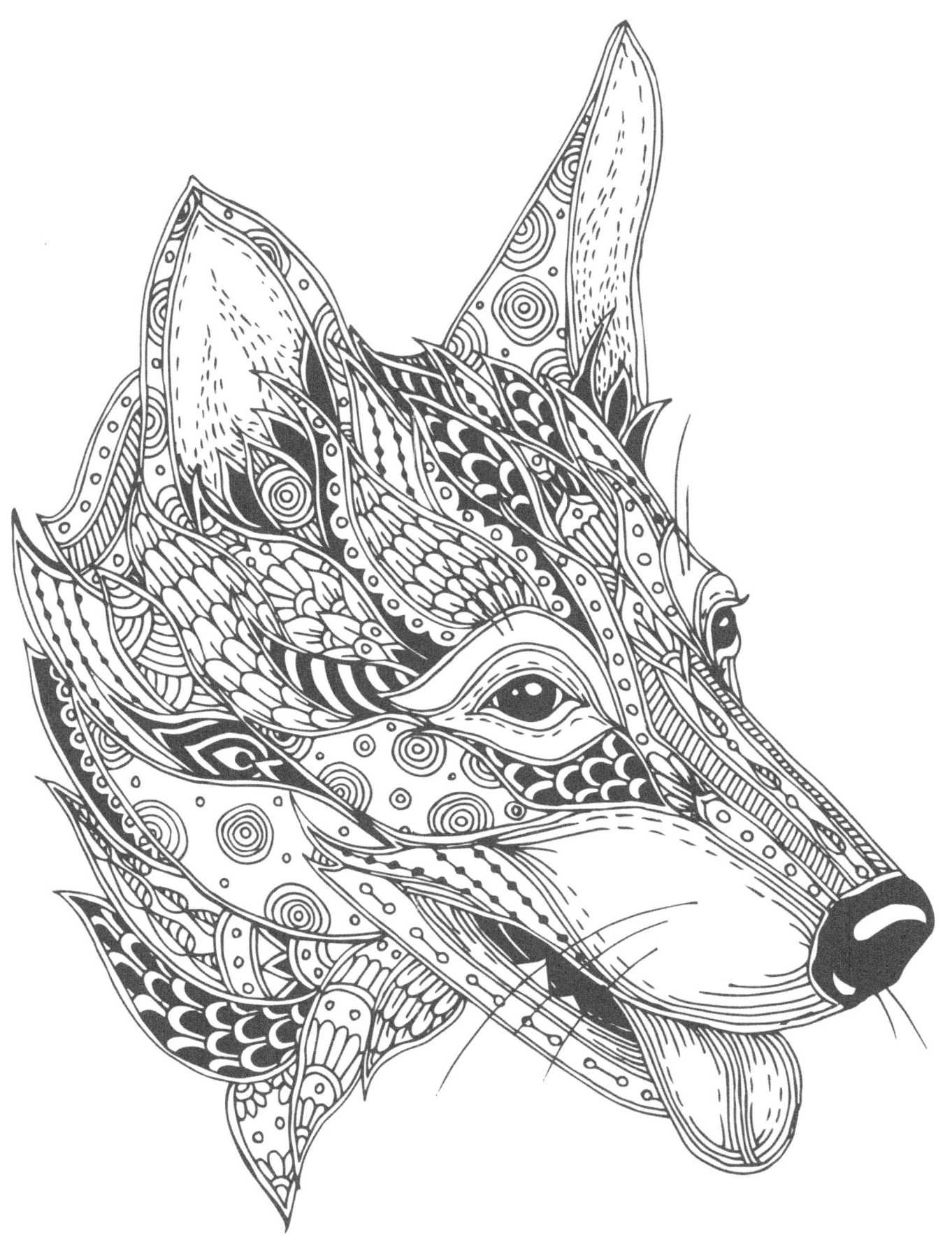

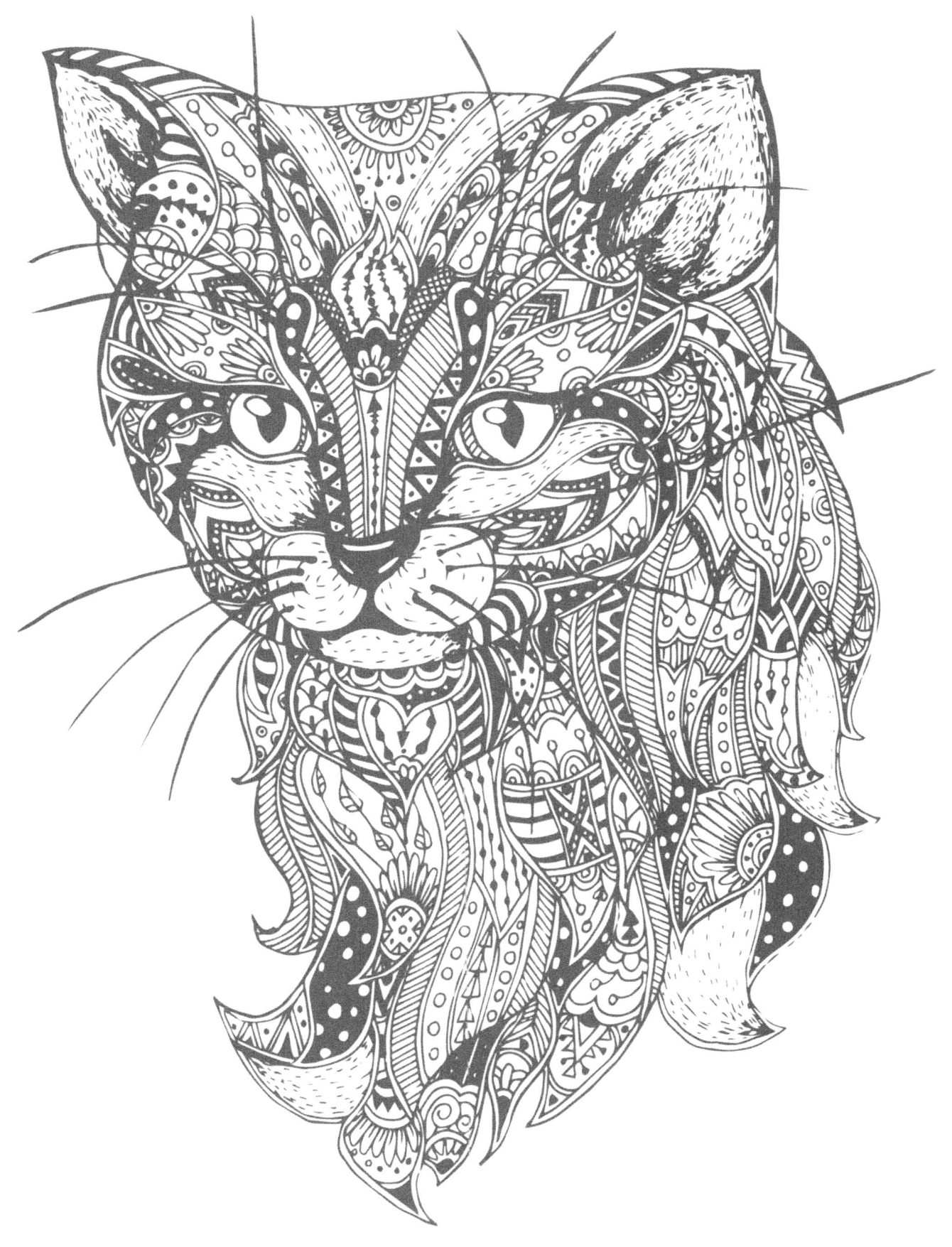

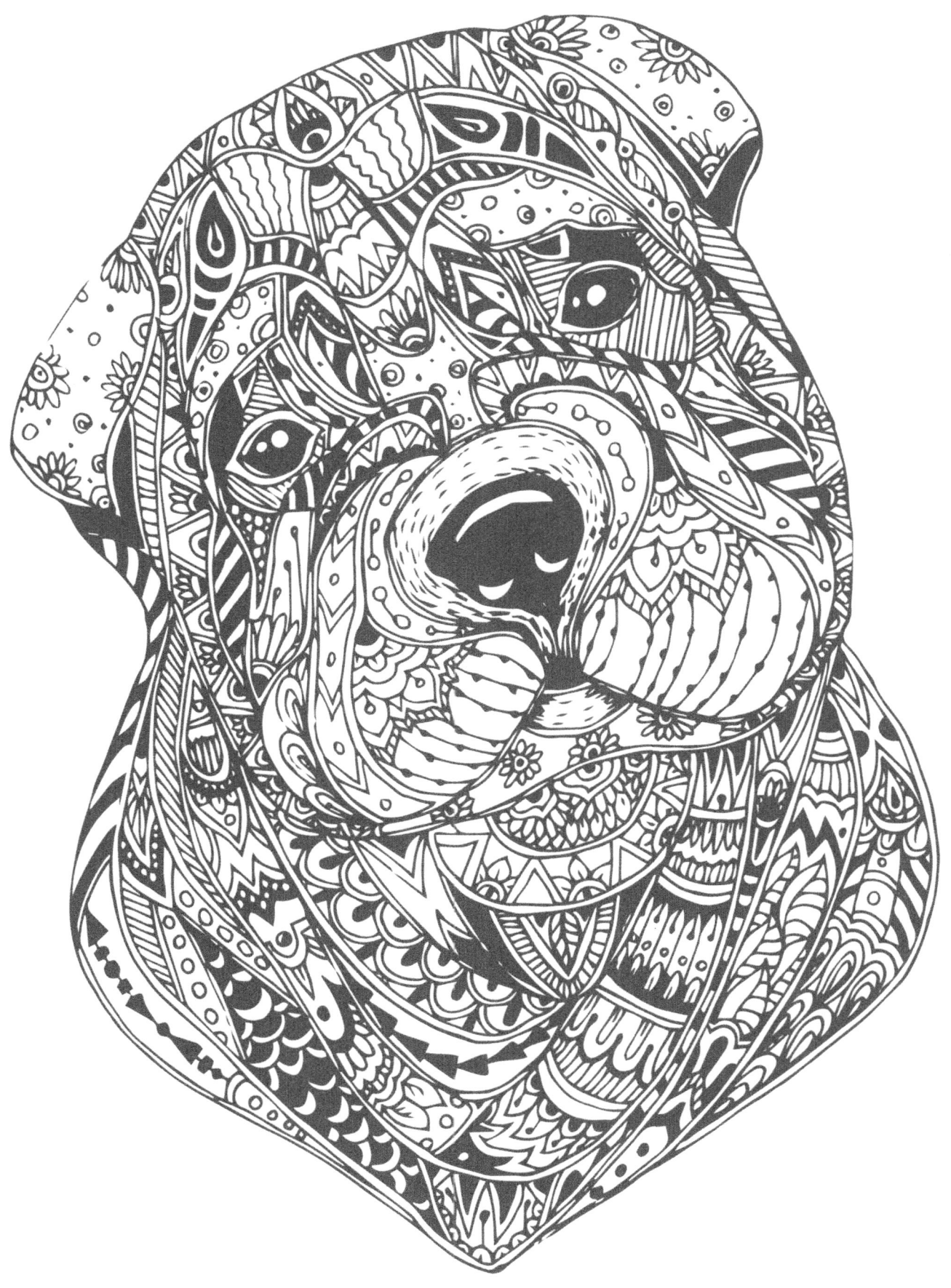

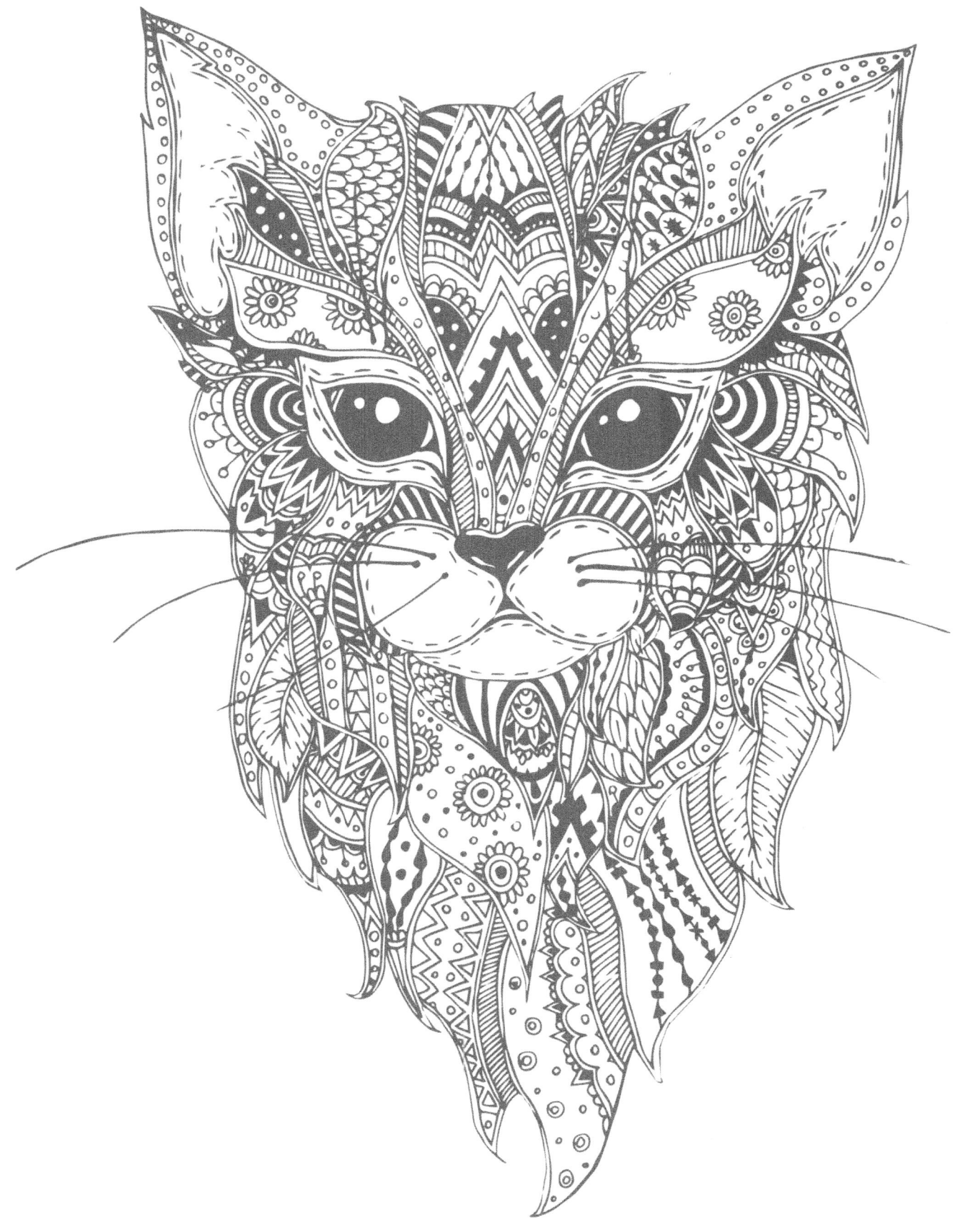

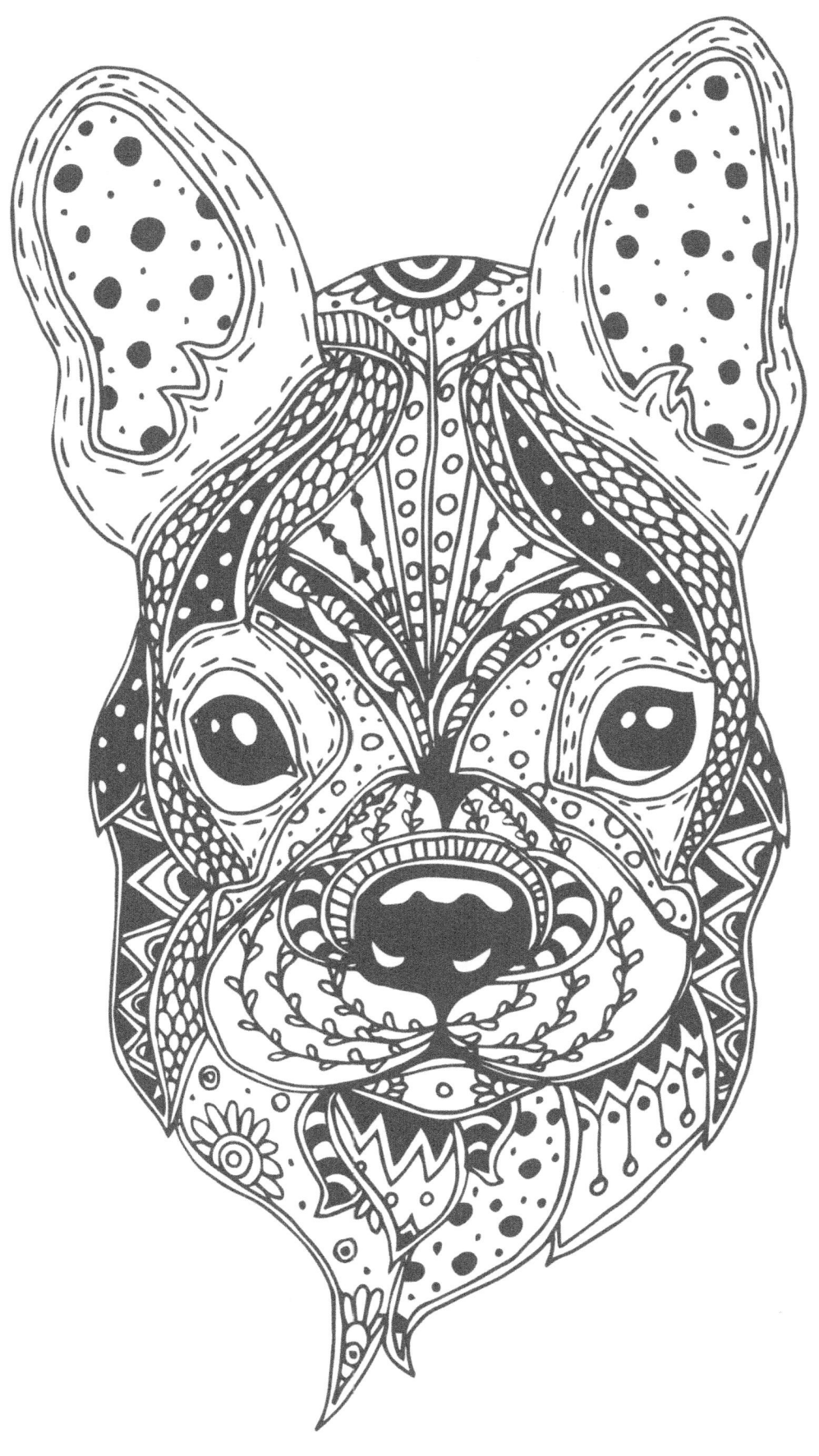

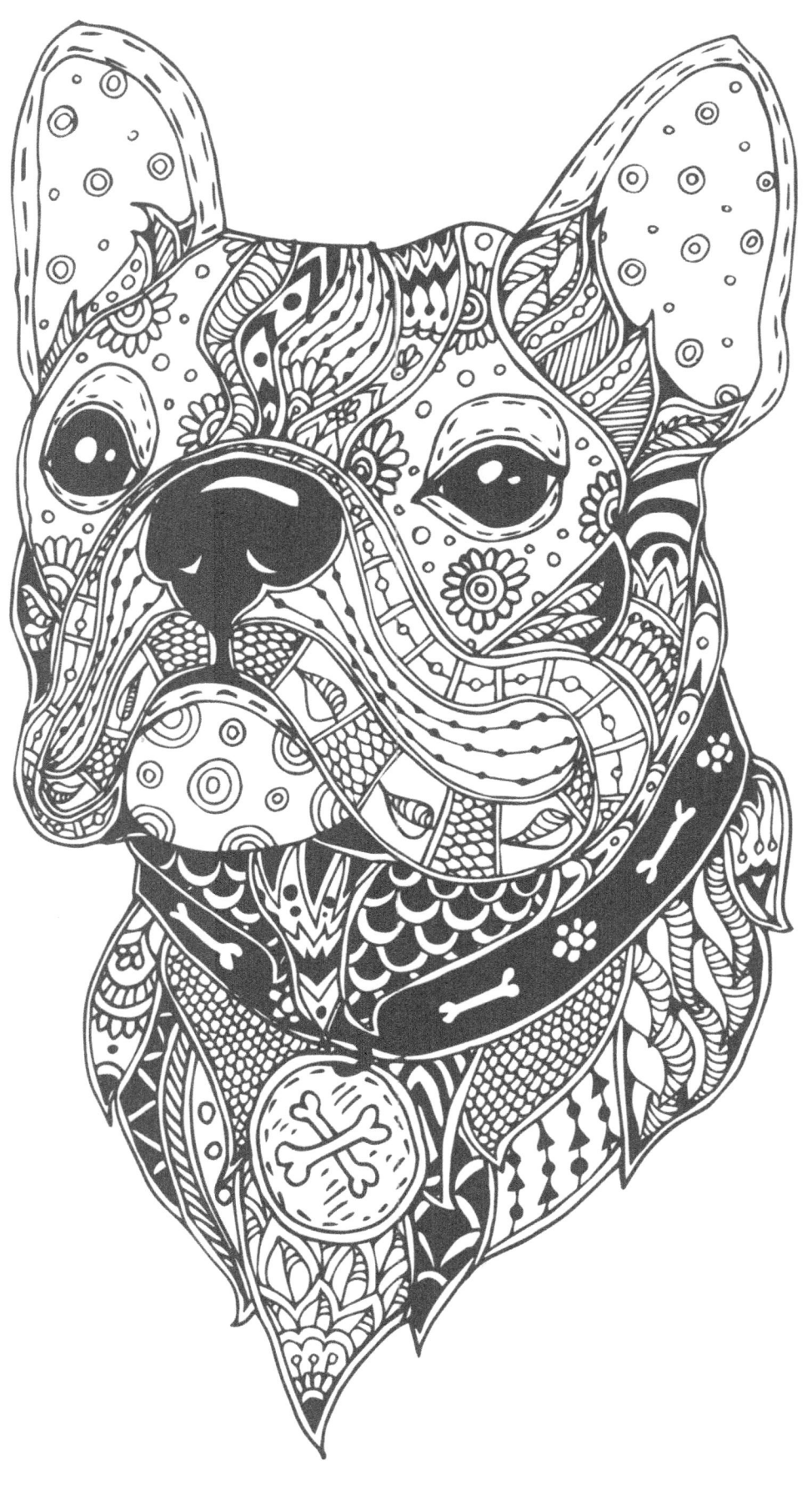

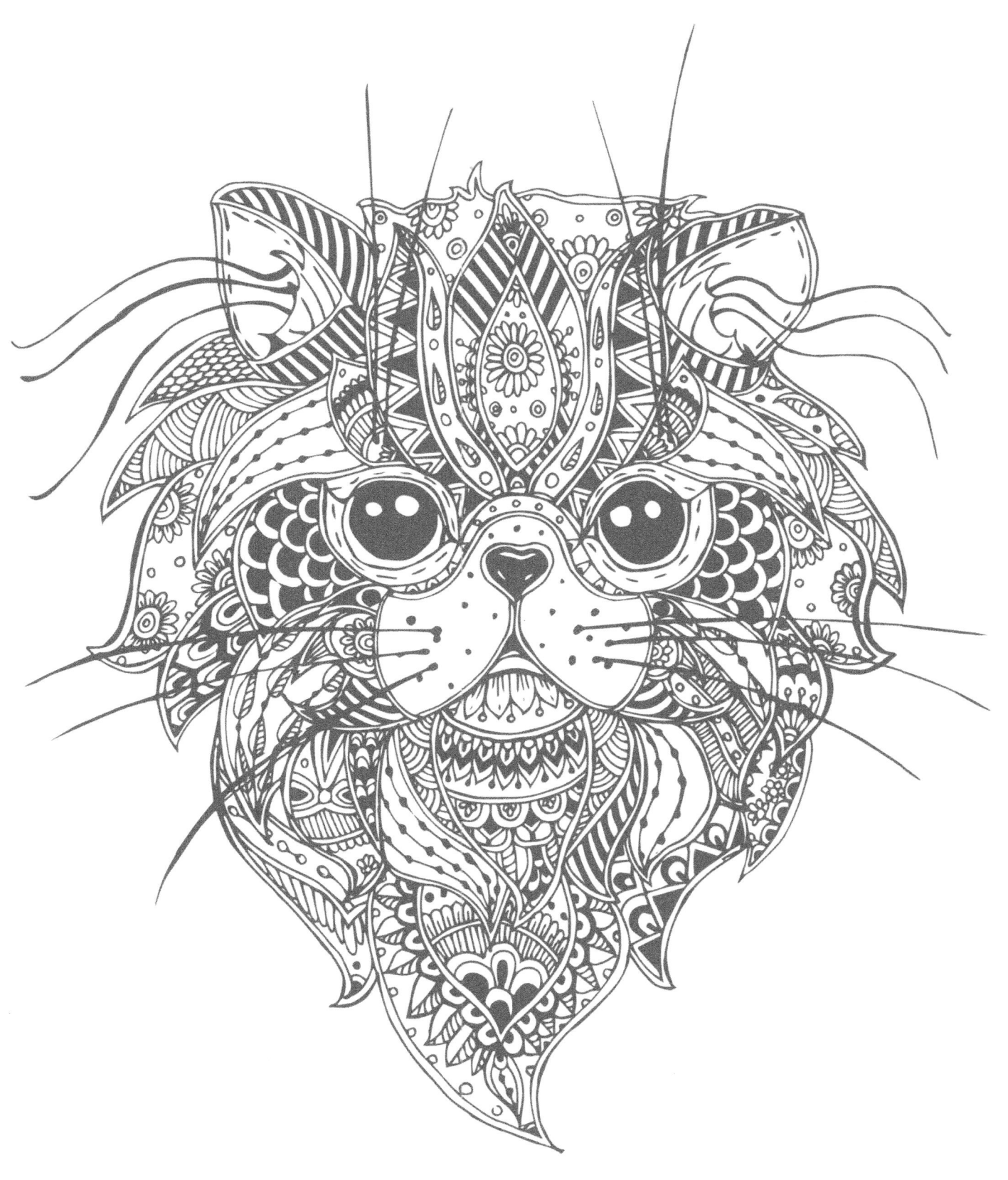

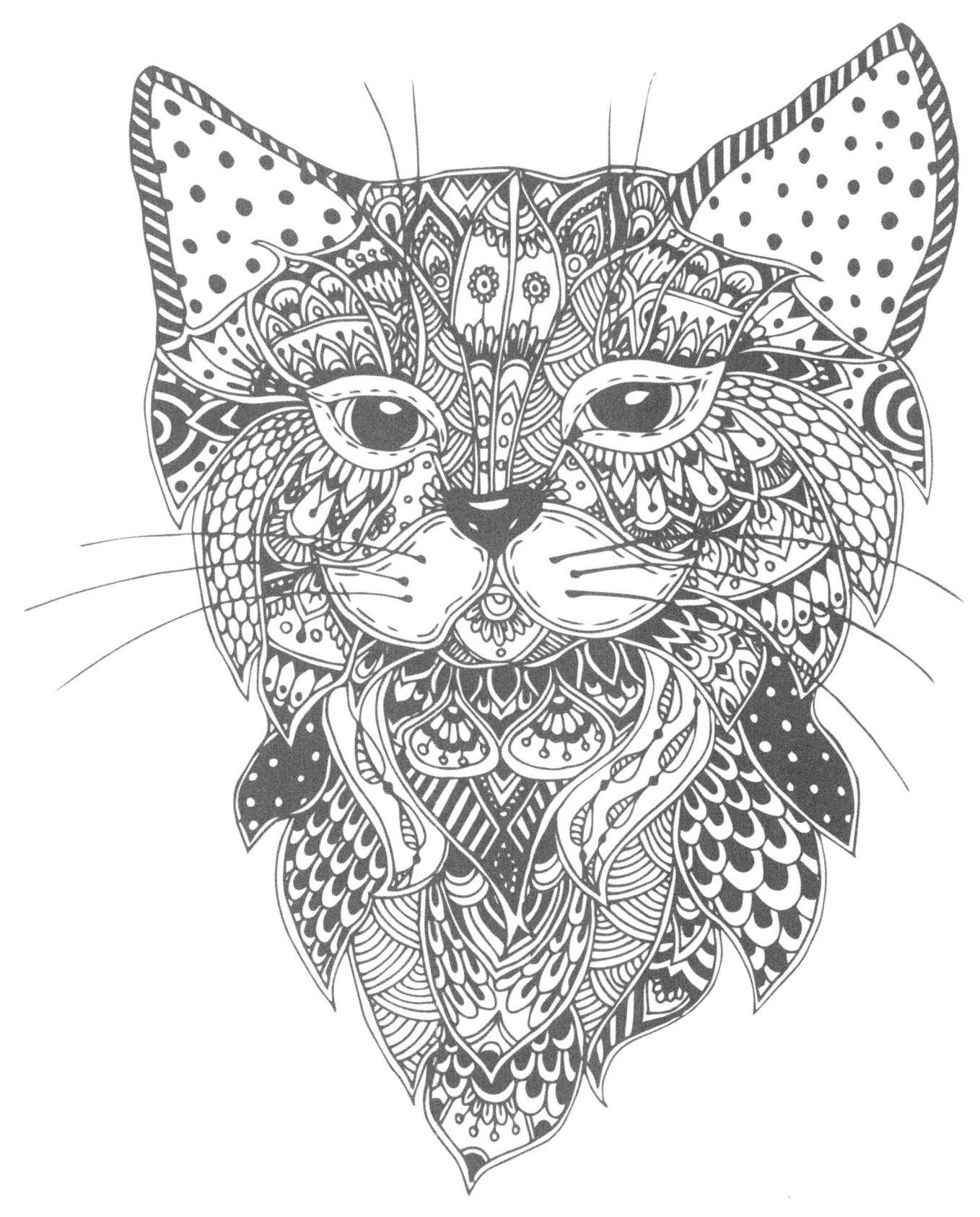

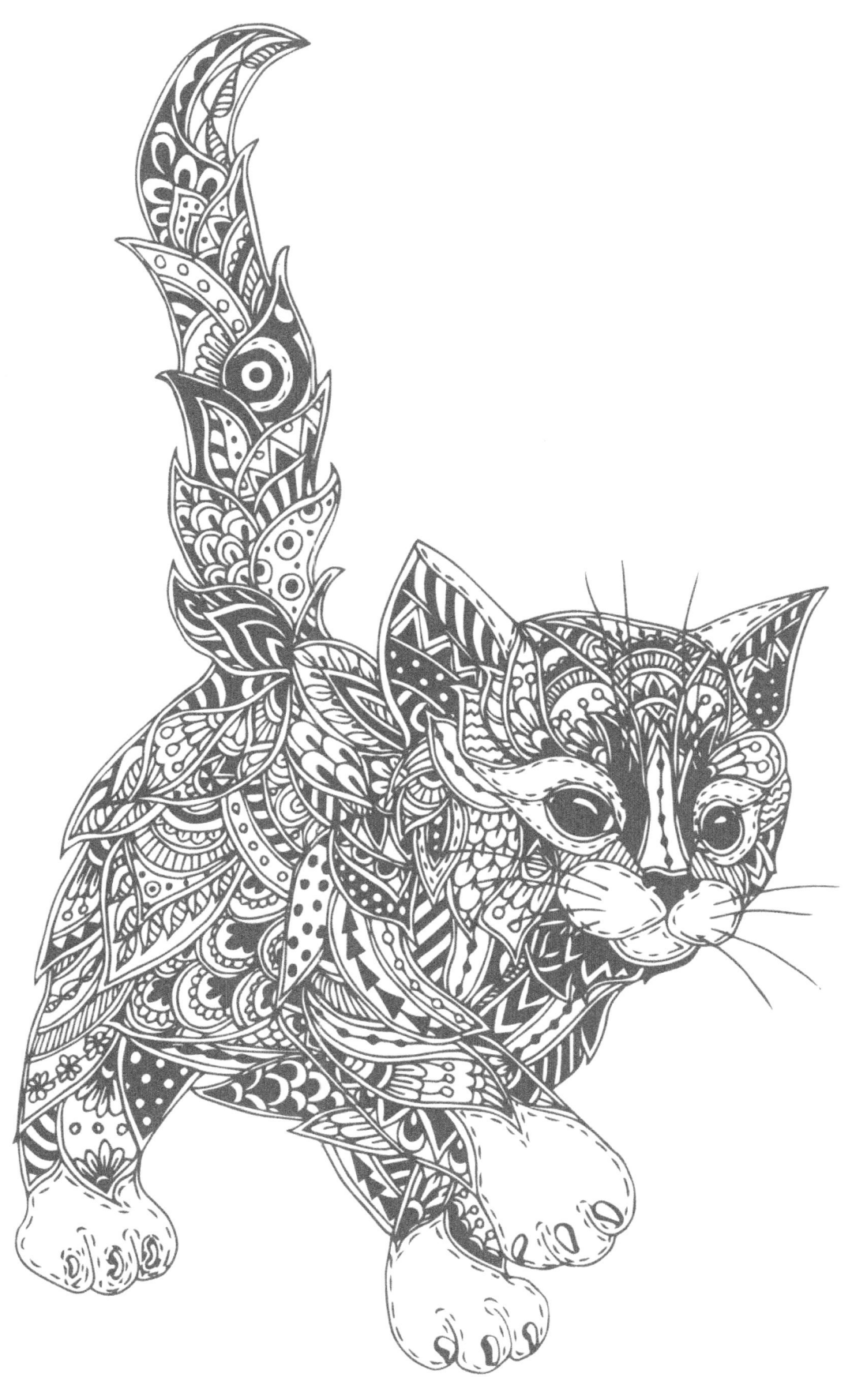

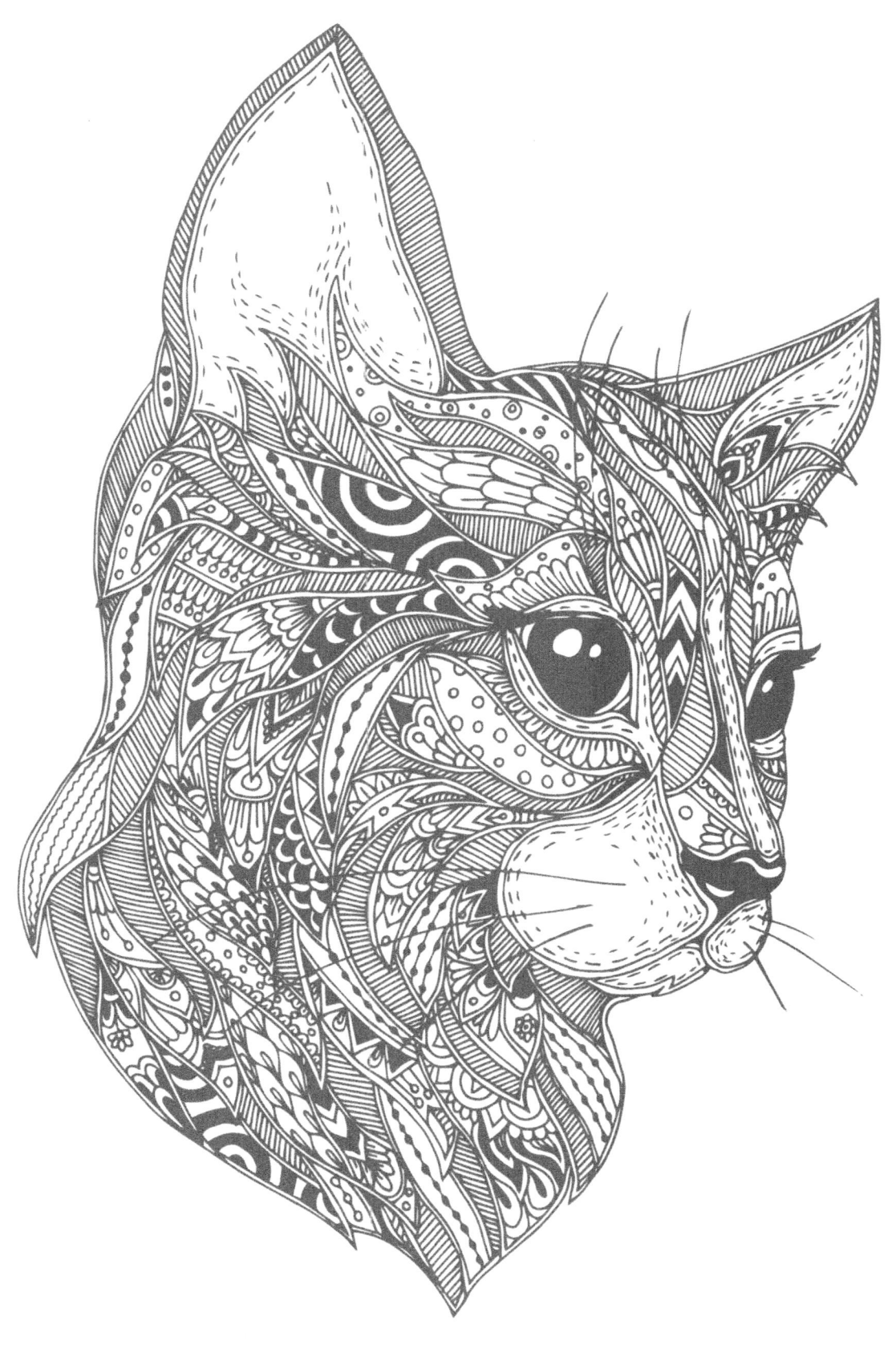

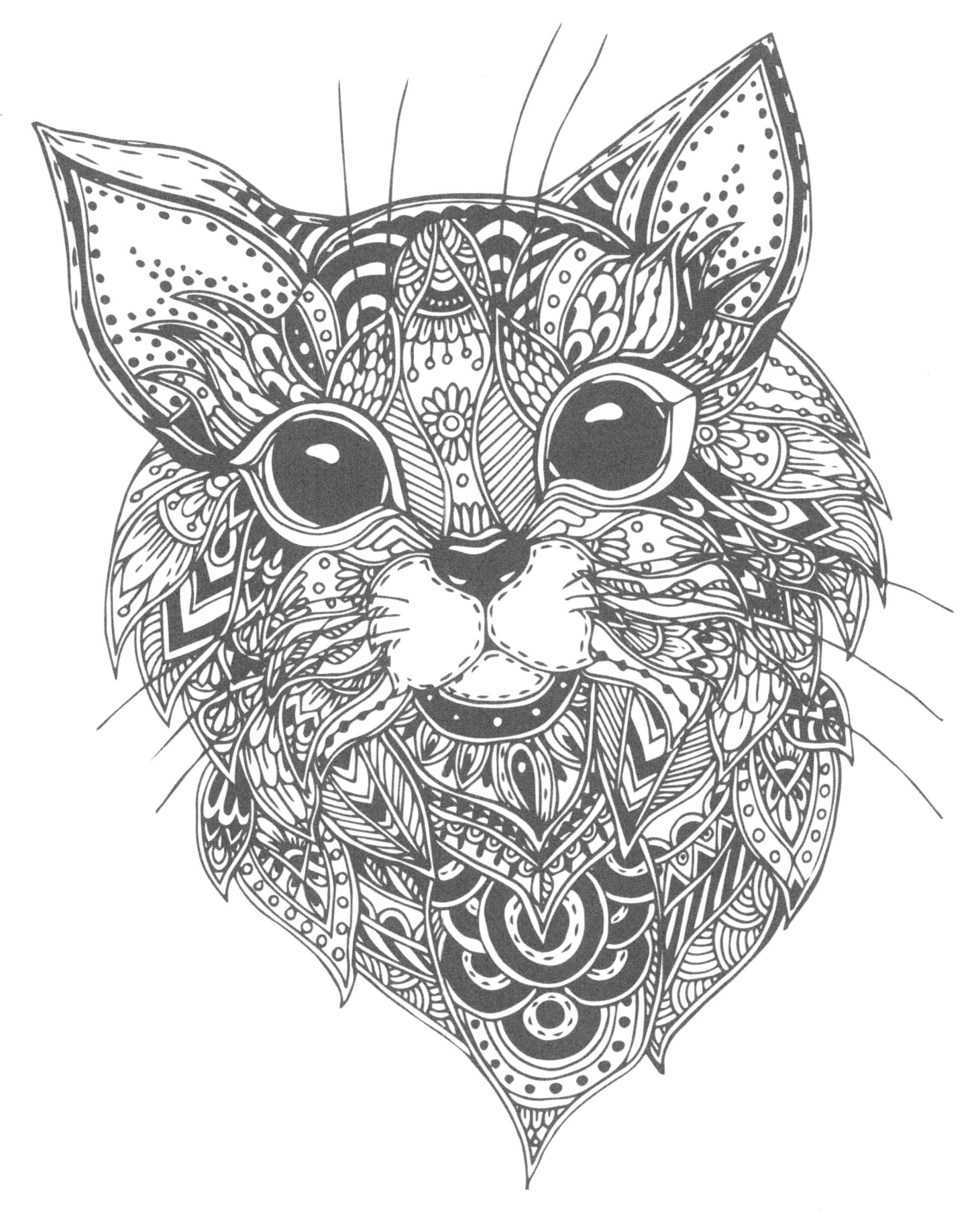

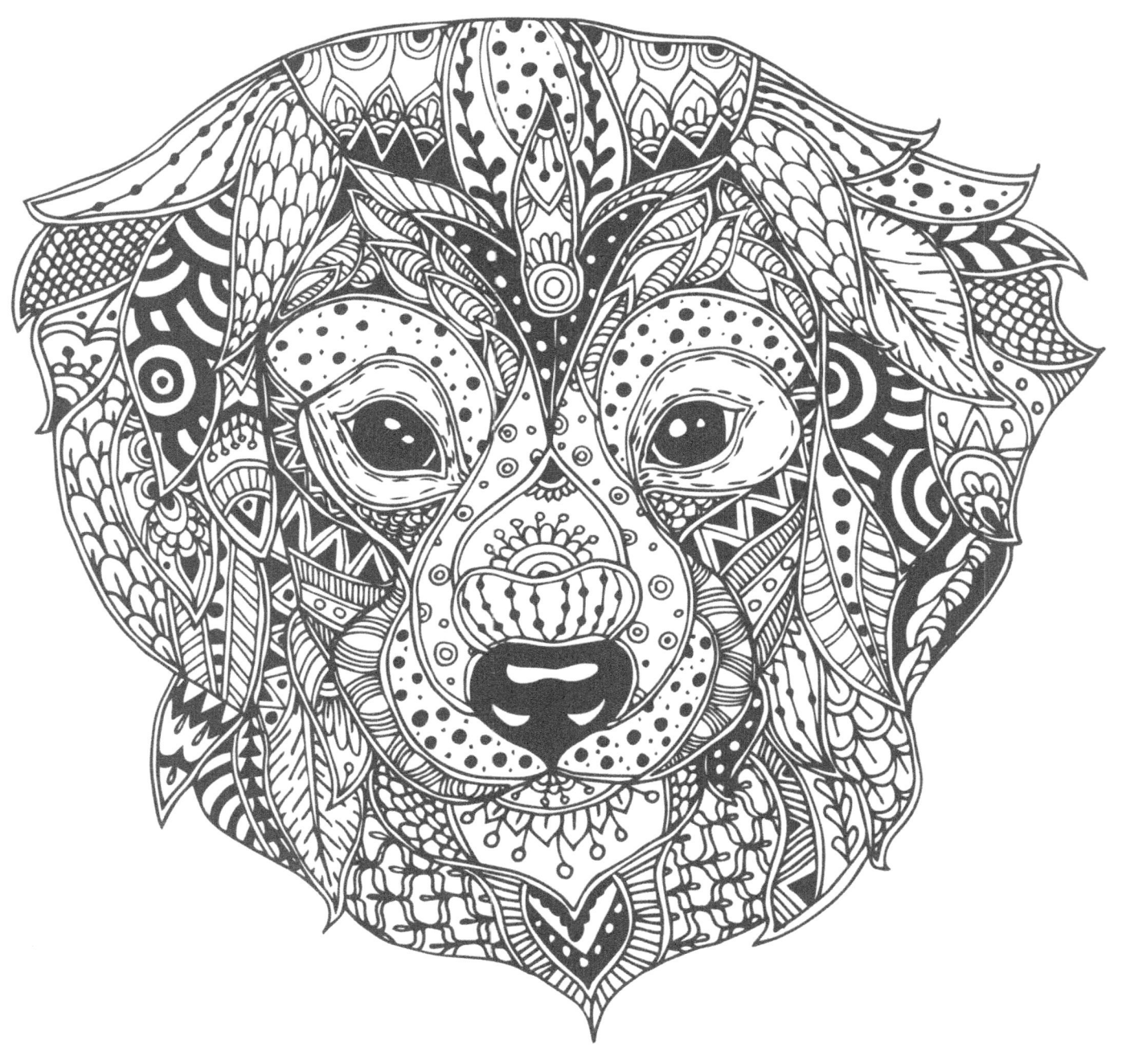

Made in the USA
Middletown, DE
28 November 2022

16243399R00038